WHEN YOU'RE READY

A Woman's Healing, From Childhood Physical and Sexual Abuse By Her Mother

by Kathy Evert

Therapist Afterword

by Inie Bijkerk

Launch Press
Rockville, MD

D0911533

Launch Press
P.O. Box 5629
Rockville, MD
(800) 321-9167

Library of Congress Catalog Card Number 87-82076

International Standard Book Number 09613205-4-0

This Book is for all those who must face such a struggle in their lives. And for all those who would support such struggling.

WHEN YOU'RE READY

contents

by Inie Bijkerk

WHEN YOU'RE READY

This volume is a record of my struggle with the most difficult thing I've had to face in my life. When I was a small child I was sexually and physically abused by my mother. It seems such a simple statement and yet it has been so enormous it has affected the rest of my life. In fact, the impact was so devastating that it was "psychologically indigestible" for 40 years. I have spent much of my life's energy blocking out all memories of what happened.

There are two books in this volume. The first book covers how I tried to cope with my memories of having been physically abused. I have always had vivid recollection of some vicious events which happened when I was about five years old. I was the youngest child of four in a poor, rural, isolated, racially mixed family with a manic depressive mother. I was born before that area of the state had electricity, indoor plumbing, running water, or good roads. It was a place and family where the Great Depression lingered for years. It was also ten years before Child Protective Services existed in that county.

My mother beat me until I could not walk. That kind of physical abuse left me emotionally damaged and became the touchstone of my anger and emotional life. When finally, in my twenties, I could begin to speak openly about what had happened, I felt enormous relief. I felt it was finally out. . . .at least to a small group of friends. . .and yet the feelings would come back, disrupt my life, and demand to be vented. It was as if my life were never quite my own. They could always rise up in me again and take control. . . .become my overriding emotional focus. But I do not believe that inner response happened because of my cultural or economic background. It happened because of the beatings. Money would not have changed that.

The second book is about what happened after I had a number of major crises in my life, in my late 30's. I was working as a counselor in a substance abuse program and within a matter of weeks one close friend left for graduate school, a second died unexpectedly of a heart attack, one of my clients committed murder and then suicide, and my mother was diagnosed with terminal cancer. I went on overload and into depression and therapy. It took an amazingly brief period of time with a good therapist to deal with my current crisis and within weeks we were slowly working backwards...back into the old pain of my childhood and towards an inevitable encounter with a wall of repression.

I discovered that I had almost no memories of anything before I was about five. It turned out that my memories of being beaten were like a cork in a bottle. On the other side of five...beyond my repressive stopper... were all the pain and memory of having been sexually abused. Breaking through that wall and into that conscious knowledge...to actually begin to live with the awareness that my mother had used me for her sexual purposes was the most devastating experience I've had in my life. It is still a thought which I find difficult to hold in my mind for very long, which remains degrading, and yet is something I can't deny. I'd like to deny it. To this day, if I could change it, if I could just make it all go away, I would give almost anything. Yet the stark reality of my experience in therapy took that option away from me. The memories and knowledge are now too conscious to repress anymore and the emotional and physical changes are too great. It's also, on the other hand, an enormous relief to have all that pent up agony released.

So, if it's so painful, why write about it, right? I think the answer to that is that I wish I'd been able to read this book myself while I was going through the process of remembering and struggling with the sexual abuse. It would have helped me feel that I wasn't going crazy. And I have yet to talk to another human being who was abused by their mother or any other female. And I have to ask why? Why are there books around about fathers or other males sexually abusing their children and yet nothing about female abusers? Is it rare? Maybe. But my gynecologist tells me he has six patients who have reported it to him to explain their difficulty with vaginal exams. Yet in talking to therapists it appears very seldom in their practice. Thinking of my own deep and heavily guarded repression of my experience I have to wonder if as a society we've now reached the point where we can talk about rape, spouse abuse, and father/male child incest, but that mother/

female/child incest is so buried that it can still only emerge in situations such as lying naked under a paper sheet in the doctor's office with someone about to touch the source of your physical/emotional/sexual agony. And even then does it emerge in a form that is recognizable or as a burst of emotion which has an unknown source? All I know is that when it did finally come out for me, it was agony and I felt I was going mad at times. So I write this partly as an act of unity with others who might find some comfort knowing that there's another end to their tunnel of despair. It is possible to get through it and be more whole. It is also important for "significant others" to know what is happening in the inner life of a person faced with such a struggle.

So this book is to share my experience. And perhaps it's one more step in my own healing process. I will not use my real name to tell you this story. I'm not ready to open my inner life for that public a viewing. This experience I've written about is still raw in some ways and I need to keep some areas of my life free from this issue. From time to time something will happen and I feel this whole thing stir in me again: the pain will rise to the surface of my consciousness and I am back at the struggle again. I am not ready to have others be free to randomly bring it up when I'm not expecting it. Some people will inevitably find me, and when they do we can make an appointment and talk. But in my personal, private life, I need to be able to be free of it.

I hope this book helps those who read it. It helped me a great deal to write it.

I need to thank a lot of people who've been supportive of me in this project. Thank you all. Especially thank you to Sherry Redding who edited the original writing and to Angie Hoogterp who helped with typing and editing.

4

BOOK ONE

I wrote the following entry in my early thirties, twenty-five years after the worst beating. Reading it now I think perhaps it was a cry of agony and anger. Originally it began with ''There is probably no way for you to understand what happened.'' Over the years that feeling has changed. Now I think others who weren't abused can learn to understand, or I wouldn't try to share this.

One day when I was five my mother's accumulated pain became stronger than her self control. She, in a rage at life, picked up a piece of firewood and took it out on me. The memory of that, the actual feeling of the physical blows landing on my body, is still as clear to me as recognizing my name or the feeling of sunshine on my face. Yet as painful as it is to recall, that beating is not the most important thing which happened that day. Long before that late winter's afternoon a process of hiding myself deep inside my child's mind and body had begun. And savage as that day was, I was probably already gone from her, and somehow her blows did not reach deep enough into my flesh to destroy my spirit. Those are the instincts of childhood that we forget as adults.

I was sitting on some firewood in the back yard and I didn't hear her coming or I would have gotten up and appeared busy. Perhaps if I had been more aware that day, my life would have been different. But I wasn't and the best I could do was start up the wood-pile towards safety.

Before I could escape she caught me by the collar of my snowsuit and in her terrible frustration she picked up a piece of the wood. The first blow, swift and strong, landed in the small of my back and drove me face first into the jumbled, harsh wood under my feet. When you are that small the breath can be quickly pounded from your lungs. I remember screaming and trying to twist loose, but soon I was simply gasping and sucking for air and getting only the taste of my own bleeding in my nose. I also recall feeling my back grow damp and hot from sweat or blood sliding down my back.

I don't know how long she hit me but it went on for a long time. After a while I could not stand and she still hit me. The funny thing is that, in the end, I couldn't feel the blows. It became more like hearing someone fluff up a feather pillow. I finally stopped struggling altogether and just passed out.

That's all I really remember about that actual beating. My ribs healed. My legs were so deeply bruised that I couldn't walk for weeks and I spent long, long days in bed alone. But I survived. Physically I regained myself and even became an athlete. But that's not the point.

The significance of the event is that on that day I became separate from all of you. I left. Like some Eskimo child who accidentally finds himself on ice which is floating away from his people, I felt the separation be permanent that day. And like the Eskimo child, I hoped and wanted to return. I felt desperate, but I was too far gone and no one could hear my cries.

In so many subtle ways you, my people, my society, lost me that day. Since that time, when you speak of ''justice'', I cannot totally believe you. When I hear people talk about doctors and speak in tones of reverence for their skills, I think of the doctor who taped my ribs and packed my nose yet never reported that beating. And perhaps most important of all, one of you gets close and says ''I love you.'' I have to struggle to believe your words no matter how much I need and want them.

An ice floe in the fog was a very lonely place to grow up and now that I am back on shore I have to try to catch up, to make all the connections I missed. My early life was put on hold, like some permanently interrupted phone call, and now even if your voice shows care and concern, I can not always hear you well. But I am alive. I did survive.

I know now that my mother could have been neatly labeled manic depressive or some such psychological term. At five I simply called her Mama. Sick maybe. After a few years I understood sick, but at that point she was just my mother.

Her ups and downs were hell. I was afraid of her from the time I can remember, even though I loved her. In kindergarten, I was afraid to come home from school because I never knew what she'd be like. Sometimes she seemed nearly dead, in an emotionless withdrawal, and she'd lie in bed staring at the ceiling, wouldn't talk, and the house would be cold and quiet. Or she might be wild in a fever of activity, stuffing the kitchen range full of wood until the chimney would glow dangerously red. She might be washing dishes, scalding them with hot water which terrified me as it splashed around. Or washing clothes, baking bread, making soup, screaming for more firewood and cutting up chickens all at the same time, and angry about all of it.

Call her anything you want, but she was who I lived with in our rural, 1940's poverty. I can recall long periods where breakfast was oatmeal, lunch was potted meat on bread, and dinner was scrambled eggs with macaroni in it. I can understand her much more now, but on that day of the worst beating I was withdrawing from her. It was her I left. She was too volatile and too dangerous; I wanted to survive.

She was in one of her frantic states the day she beat me so badly. When she wanted more wood from the pile, I got it, but I did it very slowly because the woodpile was removed from her and the kitchen. Being outdoors was safety.

Maybe I was disturbed at that point, too, I don't really know. Maybe I'd just learned to withdraw and wait her out... to protect myself from her moods. All I know is that I sat down on the woodpile and didn't hear her coming. Suddenly she was there, towering over me and raving about the wood, and the stove, and how lazy I was.

"I thought I told you to bring in that wood," she began. I'm sure I jerked to my feet when I saw her. "You start picking up wood right now if you know what's good for you! I need wood for the fire!" She was yelling. She held the collar of my coat so tightly that it was cutting into my throat and making me gag. "You never do anything to help me."

It was no use. She was so much stronger than I was that she could hit me anywhere she wanted to. I twisted and turned inside my clothes, trying to get loose. The blows simply fell. On my back, my legs. When I tried to stop her with my hands she hit them. At least one blow hit my stomach and another my right cheekbone. The muscles in my legs gave out and she hit me as I lay on the wood.

I begged her to stop. I was gasping and gagging. "You drive me crazy!" she said over and over. I was five years old. She was certainly acting crazy and I believed her. My child's mind made terrible literal connections. I was responsible for my mother's illness. I was so bad I could do that to her. In my need to believe that she really did love me, I was willing to accept that I was the one who made things go wrong. I drove her to act like that.

"You drive me crazy!" she screamed. The warm wetness grew and slid down my back. The wood made a "puff, puff" sound as she kept hitting me.

It could have been worse. I could have been killed. Some kids are.

The following entries came out of me in chunks . . . some exploding in anger, and some oozing in my consciousness like nasty stuff from a lanced boil.

I would work at this writing from time to time. I suppose it was an effort to alleviate some of the pressure caused by the larger, more painful pieces to come.

Do you know what it's like to stutter? If you do, and don't want to read any farther, I'll understand. If you don't know I can only say may god protect you from the pain.

With me it came and went with how up-tight I got. It still does if I let it. I have a standing agreement with a few of my closest friends that if they get a call from me and I can't talk they'll just keep working with me until they figure out where I am and can come to get me. It is so painful to have something to say and yet trying to say it makes your speech more difficult.

During my elementary years I was one of the smartest kids in my class, so I didn't have to talk much, and besides, the teacher I had made me feel good so I did well. But for a few years during junior high school it was terrible.

"I can-can-can-ca-ca-can't do that," I told a new gym teacher about an exercise. Everyone else in the class thought it was hilarious. I thought I was dying. "Don-don-donnnn-don't make me do that," I pleaded to howls of laughter. I thought she'd never believe I couldn't do it.

My sounds used to get right to the edge of my mouth and seal my lips with some kind of emotional cement.

"MMmmmmmmm-my. . ." God it was awful. The way I finally began to get it under control was by kicking a kid in the face who made fun of me. That stopped the teasing. Everyone knew I was crazy. I had a speech teacher in high school who talked about breathing control. I finally figured out consciously that if I tried to breathe slowly and talk slowly I could do a reasonably good job of controlling it and that built my confidence. Another thing that helped was tennis. It took a lot of tension out of me.

Where in the hell were the speech therapists when I needed them? Maybe they hadn't been invented yet.

"MMMMY MO-MO-MO-mother beat mmmmme Ww-when I was little."

That's what really helped. I was past thirty before I could say it without stuttering, and I couldn't form close relationships without saying it.

"My mother beat me when I was little." You had to know that about me.

9

Now I don't stutter except on rare occasions. When I do, when it slips out and I didn't feel it coming, I panic unless I'm with someone who knows I stutter.

Now I talk about ''writing a handbook for adults who were abused as children.''

''My mother beat me when I was little. I was just five or so. I didn't walk for quite some time after the worst beating. I've had to struggle, but I think I've worked through it now.''

Isn't that a tttr-tr-trip? I bet I could write a book better than I could t-t-ttalk it.

Sometimes when I'm at a party and people are talking about Chicago, I still want to tell about the time I spent there as a child on the north side. 2435 Bittersweet Place. I made up an aunt and uncle and I knew their apartment, what they did, things they'd say to me. . . everything.

I don't really know how it happened except I guess I just wanted it so much I created it in my mind. After things were bad with my mother, I just started thinking about what it would be like if I had a kind, loving aunt who'd come and take me away. I called her Ruth and she gave me a lot of things that I needed, like intellectual stimulation. She fed me, and talked to me a lot.

Maybe I was crazy. Who knows? No one around me understood me, and my first teacher thought I was smart, so that's what everyone else called me. But if they'd known about my imaginary Aunt Ruth and Uncle Max and all my trips to Chicago on the train they would have called me crazy.

I used to go there whenever I needed to and as I grew older I would even plan the trips in advance so I could look forward to them. I think when I was very young I truly did go off somewhere, away from being poor and isolated in the country in a family where the emotional problems were too great. And anyway it was fun. There were entire conversations I remember which were happy and even healing. If I hadn't done it -nurtured myself- who would have? I would always arrive in Ruth's presence in great conflict and feel better when I left. So she certainly did her job. And she was the only one who would talk about anything, no matter how difficult it was.

"Aunt Ruth, my mother's sick, isn't she?"

"Well, she's had a hard time, honey."

"I mean there's something wrong with her isn't there?"

She didn't speak for a while, but that was alright. When we were alone we would talk about important things, and she'd take her time, thinking things through.

"Your mother isn't well. She's had a hard time, but I'm not a doctor so I can't tell you what's wrong. She needs a lot of rest to kind of calm down sometimes."

"Do you think she's sick though, the way grandma said about her mind that time?"

"Yes, I think sometimes she's sick."

The really great thing about Aunt Ruth is that she loved all kinds of things that the rural folks I grew up with didn't understand and she encouraged those interests in me, like art. I looked at all the books on art in the library so I'd know more about it. And I did things like learn Latin words that everyone except her thought were strange. She was a strong woman. No matter how enraged I got about things, she was always stronger than I was and she would win in the end.

"I hate her, I hate her, I hate her!" I'd yell about my mother.

"You will not. I won't allow it," Ruth would say and mean it. "I'll understand if you don't love her, but you're too young to know who to hate and I won't allow it." And I was afraid I'd lose her if I let myself hate, so I'd just cry and get it out that way while we were alone and talking.

"It's O.K. to cry," she'd say. "I know how much you hurt."

Everyone else made believe nothing had happened. I loved Ruth very much.

She was smart, too, and that made it alright to read things like Shakespeare, even if I felt stupid trying to figure out what it meant.

"You're not stupid at all," she told me. It made me cry but I smiled, too. I saw her less and less as I grew older but she was instrumental in encouraging me to go to college and believed I could be a writer someday. She died when I was thirty-one.

"There's something I want to tell you," I told my close, dear friend, Shirley. "I had this Aunt, my Aunt Ruth I told you about. Well, she never really existed. I made her up. I think I needed her so that I just convinced myself that she existed."

The amazing thing is my friend understood and didn't think I was crazy. I cried and cried for a long, deep time of mourning and grief.

Sometimes I still miss her. For one thing she was funny and made me laugh. I think I get my sense of humor from her. She got me through a lot of things.

I have two things left from her. Once every year like a nice Jewish girl, I light a candle for her to mark her passing. It's proper to mourn this way.

Secondly, I have some words in my head that have always been there and I'm sure they came from her. They even sound like her.

"If it's true that the truth will set you free, then so is it true that dreams held too long and rigidly can turn on you and be a trap. Dreams are the stuff from which survival is made, but survival cannot be a dream."

I'm sure it must have been her who taught me that. No one else around me dreamed or even talked about dreaming.

We loved each other very much.

Have you ever walked down the street feeling right on top of things? You know, swimming along, feeling good...maybe on your way to a new job or to see a friend...something you feel really good about?

Well, one day after I was back in college — this was years ago — I had a day like that. I was only taking two courses, but life felt good: like it was back on the tracks and moving again.

On that particular day we had an assignment in speech class to give a brief talk using props and showing comparison. My outline was ready to hand in and I had three posters under my arm, all against the war in Viet Nam. I felt very smart because I could do what I had to do for the assignment and put on a display of my politics all at the same time. I was ready.

There was a fresh spring sun rising over my shoulder and it promised to be a beautiful day. As I went along, this young woman, about my age, was coming towards me with a child. As she crossed an intersection she carried him by one arm...something I've seen all my life...turning the kid's arm into a handle. She put him down on the sidewalk as I approached and he came along behind her...his tiny legs doing the best they could.

"Come on——!" she said to him. I don't remember the name she called him, just the tone of voice. "Come on "

He had something in his hands which distracted him and he slowed to almost a halt within a few feet.

"Come on, I said," the mother threatened with rising anger. Suddenly she grabbed his arm, and lifting him, jerked him around like a paperdoll on a string. Then taking about two steps, she swung his body directly into a metal lamp post.

"Jesus Christ!" I swore. I was within a few feet of them. I knelt partly down over the child who was screaming, gasping, rolling about and flailing his tiny arms.

I'm not sure what happened then, except that as I stood up, rage overcame me. I don't think I talked to her at all...at least not in human words. They were more like animal sounds. I remember roaring and slamming my books onto the sidewalk with terrible force and yelling and looking at the kid.

I could see fear growing in her face but I couldn't stop myself. I took three long strides and, making a fist, smashed my rage into a brick wall.

"You rotten, god damned ——"

I was wild by then and she picked the kid up as if she had to protect him from me.

"You mother ———! You bastard!" People were watching by now as she went scurrying up the street with the child rigid and screaming in her arms.

When I finally began to regain control, when I finally came down from my rage, I was standing on one of the posters. Crap.

I was almost in the classroom before I realized how much my hand hurt and that it was bleeding. I got some wet paper towels.

"What happened? Did you fall?" the teacher asked when she noticed my hand.

"Yeah," I lied.

She gave me a break and didn't call on me until near the end of class.

"See this poster? See this poster? Compare this poster. Posters started during the French revolution. End of speech."

No stuttering. No anything. Just turn it off and do what you have to do.

My hand healed in about a week except for some infection on one knuckle that left a small scar. I hear the teacher is still at Junior College. The kid must be a teenager by now. Maybe. I'd handle it differently now because the law's clearly on my side and I'm stronger, too. I'd follow her. . .get a license number. . .something. But back then I deliberately walked a different way to class after that.

My skin has healed but there's still a hole in my soul large enough for me to look through and sometimes see that child's face gasping as she carried him away.

When I was twenty-one I had spinal surgery. The pain was terrible. It felt like fire was running down my legs and they had me in traction for days. Every time I got up it would start again.

The surgeon, a really good looking man whom you might think was stuck on himself and insensitive, had a thousand X-rays and other tests done. When they were all complete, he took me into a room in the hospital and showed them to me.

"See this...and this...and this line here. Those are all places where there were breaks. What happened? Were you in some kind of accident when you were young?" He didn't press too hard and gave me room to respond however I could.

You know what I told him? Nothing.

A few years later, when I was more settled and strong enough to really think some things through, a piece of floating chipped bone in my spine lodged between the vertebrae and a disc, putting pressure on a nerve. The pain was intense and no matter whether I was up or down, it hurt day and night. I was back in the hospital, spent days in traction, but this time I had a different surgeon.

I lay there all those painful days and thought, why did she have to use a piece of firewood? I wondered how bad my back would get.

This time the emotion was right at the surface and I wanted to ask a lot of questions but I didn't know how to raise them and maintain my self control.

And do you know what this surgeon asked? Nothing.

As the years went on I found myself needing to move farther and farther away from my family emotionally. Yet at the same time I was terribly unresolved by the events of the past and my feelings towards them. Whenever my family would contact me I'd respond. I'd hope that somehow this time I could be who they wanted. That I could be accepted and valued.

It never worked out that way and I'd withdraw again. It never got put back together again and more and more I looked elsewhere for comfort.
  But in the end you grow up, get married, have kids, friends. . .the whole thing. And still when the phone rings there's something in you that makes you try one more time. You keep trying to be the "good child" because somehow maybe they'll become the "good parents."

Twenty-five years later and he calls me. Can you believe that? He calls me. . .twenty-five god damned years later.
  "Hello? Kathleen?"

No one calls me that anymore except them. When I was born my mother refused to name me and told my dad he had to do it. I heard that story all my life. He thought I looked like one of the Dionne quintuplets and he wanted to name me after one of them but he couldn't remember any of their names. I could have been "Cecile" or "Yvonne".
  "What's wrong?" I asked. . .my free hand reaching for Jim in the darkness.
  "Your mother. . .she took some pills. I didn't know it until she got sick."
  My body jerked and Jim woke up. "What's wrong?"
  "Where are you?" I asked.
  "At the hospital."
  I was trying to see the clock. . .trying to find something that made sense. What the hell time is it anyway? 12:30 A.M.
  "I'll be right there."
  The late winter air was cold and raw as I ran from the house. Christ! Now this, too? Stay calm. Just try to stay calm. Have some control.
  He was standing near the end of a hallway looking drawn and ashen. His back and the palms of his hands were pressed against the wall and his eyes looked vague when I touched his shoulder.
  "Dad? Is she alright?"

Nothing.

"Is she in there?" I said, indicating a door. Silence. I opened the door and there was a nurse standing over my mother, taking her blood pressure. The room felt hushed and still.

"Are you her daughter?"

I nodded my head.

"She's still sick. Will you be with her for awhile? Good. I'll be back in twenty minutes. Call me if you need anything."

I inched closer until I could touch the bed railing which had been raised around her. She looked puffy and swollen and her head rolled from side to side. She mumbled a couple of times. There was a small pan by her face to catch vomit. Pale. Very pale and wilted.

Stay calm, I thought. The cool metal railing in my hands held me in place. Now what? I walked to the window after a while and looked out into the darkness. Why does everyone else get to sleep tonight? A Gideon Bible lay hunched and lurking on the window sill.

"Thou shalt honor thy mother and thy father that their days might be long upon the face of the earth," it whispered.

Crap. Would it be wrong to look that page up and flush it down the toilet?

I went back out in the hall to my father. No use. He just hung there—immobile on the wall. He was stuck to it like some dried up, chewed up cud of discarded bubble gum. Stay calm. Just keep your cool.

When I went back in she was moaning and I went close to see. I held on to the railing for stability and as I watched she began to seem a little pathetic. She rolled her head around and moved her hands as though she were trying to stay afloat on the sheets.

She might die, I thought. No one has said she wouldn't. I wonder if she's dying. That was a fascinating idea and I watched intently, and moved my hands up and down the smooth railing.

It seemed like a long time passed but she didn't get any worse and my hands tightened on the rail. I gripped the metal as if it had some responsibility to carry out and perhaps my deadly

17

clinch on its throat would make it act on her.

You won't die, will you, I told her silently. You'll just lie here puking for a few hours, moaning and groaning and feeling sorry for yourself. Look at you. A full meal of sleeping pills and the only results are puke in your hair and you stink. Everyone else will go insane.

Stay calm. Just try to keep it together, I kept telling myself.

A terrible force grew in my forearms. This is me, ma, I thought. I'm grown. My hands are big now and my arms are strong. God damn you. All my life you've made me hurt. I was holding the railing so tight it was beginning to squirm.

There she was, defenseless. No one will know. I can pound her to within an inch of her life. She is too far gone on the pills to stop me and she can't make words. . .just sounds and gagging.

The railing had little tolerance for pain and was crying out now. Shut up, I told it. She's my god damned mother.

Somehow, in the eye of my mind, my hands left the railing and floated above my head and then with all the force of years of endurance they came down upon her. I pounded her, striking her stomach, hitting her arms and legs, beating her face until it bled. In a terrible rage I ripped the intra-venous needles from her arms and cut her off from hope. Die, you ——! Die. . . . My blows were vicious and fell on her again and again until my mind could no longer imagine it. She had it coming.

The poor railing was struggling to get free and I knew it had done nothing to deserve its fate, but was simply in the wrong place at the wrong time. A victim. It happens.

I don't know how long it took me to vent myself, but when the nurse returned I was exhausted. She came slipping silently and efficiently up on her floating nurse's shoes like some spook in the night.

She went about her work on the blood covered body as if nothing had happened. Blood pressure. Pulse. She glanced at me at the precise moment I realized the railing was dead, hanging lifeless in my hands, and I could only hope she didn't notice.

''She'll be alright now. She'll probably sleep for several hours.''

I couldn't move and I couldn't speak. My god, I've killed the railing, I thought. Can't she see the blood? How can she miss it?

She looked at me suspiciously for a moment. "Why don't you take your father for a cup of coffee? We'll take care of her. You look tired."

I'm covered with blood and she thinks I look tired! She started around the bed towards me. Don't let her touch the railing I thought. She'll know it's dead.

"Don't touch me," my voice said as she got to the foot of the bed. "Don't come near me."

She stopped abruptly. "Alright," she said in nurse talk. "But I think you'd better sit down."

"Just don-don't touch me," I said, making her keep her distance. "Stay away."

"I'll be right back," she said and left. I tried to get my hands loose from the railing. Just put it down, I told myself. It's dead. I hadn't meant to kill it. I just had. Just feeling my anger toward my mother had killed it. It was so limp and lifeless when I let it go. She'd had it coming but that poor railing hadn't done anything to me. It was just trying to help. I began to panic. Maybe they won't find out it was me who killed it. Stupid! Everyone will know. They'll know just by looking at me. They'll know how terrible I am to feel that anger.

There was nothing more to do in the room so I went back to the hallway to see my father. He was still standing there, only now one foot was raised and the sole of his shoe was pressed against the wall. Maybe that's what to do. Maybe the wall had strength and I didn't know it. I took a position beside him and leaned against the wall. At least I could stand up. I'll just wait for the nurse to come and get me for killing the bed rail. I felt bad about that, but my mother had it coming.

She lived. She woke the next day and cried for hours. There was no sympathy in me. My father was a ghost.

Later he said he was grateful I'd been with him and that she thought I cared because I'd been there that night. Shit. She was in the hospital three days and I never touched her.

I was never charged with strangling the bed railing. The staff at that hospital is apparently poorly trained and couldn't tell the difference between a dead railing and a live one. To this day they don't know what happened. But I was deeply ashamed.

When I think about some of the professionals in the child abuse field I have strong feelings. I want to tell them how I see things from this side of the fence.

I've read your books. I've read about how you see the problem. "It's a disaster," you say. "Terrible. An epidemic that's raging and no one cares. Why can't we stop it with our skills?" You say you talk with each other and you can't figure it out. Just can't get a handle on it, huh?

Well, let me explain it to you. You weren't there. And now, years later, there may be no way for you to understand the deadening isolation of abuse. You think you know, but you don't. Unless you were beaten, or told from the earliest time you could understand that you weren't wanted, or you can remember how it felt to have an adult probe and enter you sexually before you weighed fifty pounds, you don't know. Not really.

For you to understand, for anyone to understand, you'll have to get in touch with at least the tip of this iceberg. Close your eyes. Imagine you're shrinking...shrinking, getting smaller and smaller until you begin to feel tiny and vulnerable. Allow your mind to make you so small that all dogs look huge, the front porch seems far above the ground, and the shadows on your bed at night look like snakes and bears. Try to remember again how small you were.

I don't know how big I was at the time. I was only about five, so I couldn't have weighed more than forty pounds. Maybe fifty. I stood about as high as my mother's waist.

Now, imagine yourself in a strange, huge mansion where the windows reach the ceiling and you have to crawl up onto the furniture. It's quiet and still until suddenly a huge adult comes in to menace you. He or she looks huge and hulking and screams at you and pounds the furniture in rage and disdain. And you don't know what's wrong. Why is there screaming? What have you done? Feel it. Imagine a slap to the face under such circumstances or a blow to your back which takes your breath away. Or how about if this huge person picks you up, throws you against the wall, and as you slide to the floor he kicks you.

When it's over you're hurt. You cry and try to make sense of it. Is it really over? The rest of your stay in the mansion is spent with other people who act as if nothing ever happened. They don't ask you how you were bruised or why you've been crying. They only ask things like is your homework done? Did you feed the dog?

On a seemingly random basis, the crazy adult occasionally returns. Sometimes he or she beats you, or sometimes just stares at you silently or maybe screams and raves about things that make no sense to you at all.

"You think that calf is so nice, huh? Well, I hate it here and it wasn't my idea in the first place. Your damn grandmother can have those dishes for all I care. And I'll tell you something else. I'll tear those flowers up myself!"

It might go on and on. No one offers you hope. You keep looking for the ones who will help but they never do. There's so much you can't comprehend and you put too much of your childhood energy into trying to make sense of your life....thinking about things you shouldn't have to think about. Children need time and energy to play in order to grow and flourish. You may spend some of your time figuring out how to move so your broken ribs don't hurt too much.

"Keep the tape on for a week and a half and let her stay in bed. I'll take the stitches out when you bring her back in."

Professional? Shit. He never did a damn thing.

Keep remembering how tiny and vulnerable you've become. You're physically hurt and you don't even have the right to decide to take aspirin. You're a child, remember? You long ago gave up thinking you could tell how adults would treat you. You no longer know who will hit you, scream at you, or mock your need for human warmth and comfort. You're afraid to talk, and after a while you're afraid you can't talk. You're too young to understand the concept of human spirit or dignity, but you know when something inside is breaking. You know part of you is dying and you have no power to stop it.

Once when I was older I talked to a minister about it.

"Well, don't be angry. She couldn't help herself. It's up to you to find it in your heart to forgive her this sin."

I was about eleven at the time and he told me it was my responsibility to deal with it. He didn't do anything either. Professional, my ass.

If you really want to know about child abuse, if you have the guts, gather your human determination and stamina and stay in this little experiment until you finally feel so small and beaten that you know you can no longer control the shrinking of your self. You, the person you might have become, just keeps getting smaller and smaller. You hide deeper and deeper within your body, until the conscious you, the part that has to deal with reality, almost totally loses contact with even your insides. You're nearly gone. You almost no longer exist as a person.

When you try to make sense of this situation you find yourself taking responsibility for things you could not control.

"Maybe if I was different," you tell yourself. "I just wish somehow I'd found a way to be so she would have loved me. At least a little bit."

When you've reached this point where you'll do anything, even blame yourself to gain some bit of hope, go without sleep for about a week. Let yourself get half crazy from exhaustion until you keep thinking over and over about the people who hit you, and the ones who might have helped you, and you don't know why they didn't. Keep thinking about why no one ever loved you the way you wanted/needed them to. Let your mind wander and whirl through useless circles and you'll begin to get a feel for the problem.

Now, lock yourself in a closet, exhausted and ashamed that you're so totally out of control and unlovable. Sitting there in the darkness ask yourself a thousand times "Why me? What did I do? Why don't they love me?"

Ask it again and again. Over and over. Try to make sense out of not feeling loved. You'll never find an answer that gives any real comfort. Cry until your tears are gone forever.

You're lost now. Just float along as best you can. Ten years? Fifteen? It doesn't make any difference. Float. Stay detached. Feel your adolescence and early adulthood slip away.

But there's one more danger for you to face. Suppose you become vaguely aware that there's a tiny being in the closet with you. A child. And if this baby is to survive at all it will be because you care for it. You will be totally responsible. It is tiny and helpless the way you once were.

Now, professionals, ask yourselves where child abusers come from. That they come from having been abused is a damned simple answer. If you really were in our imaginary closet, how would you respond to this child's dependence? Be honest. No textbook tricks.

Where does strength come from when your spiritual well is dry? Where do gentleness, nurturing, and love come from when you've never known loving, growth-producing care? How do you learn to show compassion before you experience it yourself?

"One thing I have is I remember the touch of her hands on my face, brushing my hair from my eyes, before she got sick. I have that. But when she. . . .well, I just wish I'd known how to be so she would have loved me." I've said that/thought that a thousand times.

Get in touch with how fragmented and cut off the whole experience can leave you. Try to be an adult twenty four hours of every day when you lost your own childhood. You'll find after a while you may prefer the closet and will retreat there occasionally for secret, shame filled rituals of guilt and despair. Why did it happen in the first place? You ask it over and over. It makes you very weary.

One day when I was twenty-seven years old I was driving alone down a highway on a lovely summer afternoon when I realized I was idly thinking "If I had just brought in the wood. Maybe if she hadn't gotten so angry she wouldn't have gotten sick. Maybe if. . ." I caught myself. Twenty-seven damned years old and I'm still trying to take responsibility for what someone else did.

You think that's crazy? Listen, I figured something else out, too. No one, not one single soul, professional or not, ever told me "Hey, it wasn't your fault. You didn't do anything to deserve that."

Think about it. You and your public service announcements that tell me I'm going to be an abuser. Twenty-seven years and no one has said the thought process you used as a child to try to cope was faulty. Think about all the women who were never told there was nothing they could have done at four years old that was seductive to their own daddy. No one ever told me it was impossible for me to make my mother crazy. No one ever told me there was nothing I did that deserved that kind of abuse.

"You drive me crazy," she had screamed over and over. Where was the voice that told me anything different? It takes a long time to come back from such a far and painful place. A long time.

"O.K. This won't take long," she said as she began. "We do a brief intake interview to try to understand your child better."

It takes a long time.

"And let's see....any history of bedwetting?" "No."

"Disturbed sleep?"

"Just dreams."

"Stuttering or other speech problems."

"NNNNNNo."

"O.K. Fine." she smiles. "I think that's all we need to talk about. Everything seems fine."

Professional. SSSSure.

I'm not saying there aren't real professionals. There are. Thank god there are lots of good people. But Abraham Maslow, god rest him, said some folks get stuck with holes in their souls that they can't fill in themselves. There are some things which have to come from outside yourself, things you can't do for yourself. How can you mother yourself even after you know that's what you need? There are some things like having another human being look at you with loving eyes that you can't do for yourself no matter how hard you try. No one told me I couldn't make my mother crazy. But also no one ever said I couldn't make her well and whole and caring, or make her put her hands on my face again the way I remember when I was very young. Abe Maslow taught me that.

And Carl Rogers says there are very few therapists who are really good at working with insanity. He says it's too scary to really get in touch with someone else's craziness because you can't tell after a while where their craziness leaves off and yours begins. Perhaps it's the same with pain and that is why there is so much silence.

Well, anyway I'm doing alright. But still I guess I have to ask. Who among you can look at such pain? Who will not just label

25

me as a potential abuser but will really see me and understand how far away I have gone from you? You would not have to actually touch me, but who among you would have spiritually touched my face?

First of all I want to say I do not believe in devils, people being possessed, or anything like that. Just keep that in mind. I'm not crazy either. At least I don't think so and no one has told me I am lately. It's just that when I was young, too young, a part of me shrank so small that it got sort of displaced in my body and hid in me for years.

I know this sounds crazy, but I think the part of me that was a child just became too frightened to go on, and being so reduced in size and power, it took up a fearful, guarded residence in my chest. . . . somewhere near my bronchial tubes to be exact.

The reason I know that it existed is that whenever I'd get really scared and my chest and breathing would tighten, that is where my fear would come from, where my basic human cries originated. In order to explain it, even to myself, I always thought of it as ''my little person''.

I've never been afraid because the little person was living in me. From the time I was very young I knew it was there and I knew that it wanted to come out someday. I could feel it very close to the surface of my body at various times as I grew up, but it never directly exposed itself to anyone and would probably still be hiding in me except that I told Shirley.

Shirley is my good friend. . .the first truly adult relationship I managed to form. I was about thirty at the time, and I had lots of friends, good friends, but somehow she and I made a commitment to be real with each other. . .to be honest in a fundamental sense. It made me nervous at first. I told her about what had happened when I was young and she didn't go away. I confessed my fears of being unlovable, and she still didn't go away. She even went back with me to the house where it all happened, met my parents, and she stayed with me. But most of all she helped me learn what it feels like to have someone love you just because you are who you are. . .a person.

That may sound stupid, but I had to learn that and she was my best teacher.

We talked and talked. I told her all the things I'd felt but could never say. I stuttered and she didn't go away. She said we would know each other for a long, long time, so if there were things I couldn't say now it was O.K. because someday I would say it all and it would be done. That allowed me to say much.

Sometimes I would cry and cry and she didn't go away. Great sighs came up from within me and it became easier for me to feel love from other people and I entered a happy period of my life. The tenderness of the first days, the shy feelings of being open to people, are still in my memory.

After all the years of feeling so alone and isolated, I began to feel like a baby whale washed up on an Oregon coast with people coming to see if they could help. It seemed like people wanted to provide the things which would make survival and growth possible. I didn't always understand why they were kind and loving to me, but I learned to accept it and slowly I began to feel that I belonged somewhere where people wanted me. It was the spring of my life.

One day Shirley and I were talking and I suddenly told her about the little person. I could feel the little person growing in me and I wanted to tell her.

"I know this sounds crazy, but all my life I've felt like there was part of me that nearly died . . . and it just got smaller and smaller and it's been hiding inside me all this time like a tiny little person."

"What do you mean?"

"I really don't know except that it's there. It's the part of me that was hurt too much when I was young, I guess. Only now I feel like it's getting bigger and bigger and I'm getting a little scared because there's really not room in here for both of us."

"What do you want to do? Do you want the little person to come out?"

"I think so, only that's crazy, isn't it?"

Just thinking about it made me edgy and part of me wanted to leave, to run from the words which exposed that idea.

"Then let it out," she said before I could escape.

"I cccan't . . . I don't know how."

"Where is it?"

I put my hand on my upper chest and it tightened and grew tense. She'll think I'm crazy, I thought. I'd better go.

But Shirley is a very wise woman. She simply reached over and touched that same spot and drew her hand back as though she'd taken hold of something and I felt like she'd pulled some psychic cork in my soul. Emotion poured from me. I cried. I laughed and laughed like a little kid excited about taking a trip or a new puppy. I smiled and smiled like I think I'd never smiled. Phewwww. . .it felt like the windows had been thrown open at the end of winter.

I couldn't really talk, but I wasn't stuttering.

"It's O.K.," Shirley said. "Now the little person's free." Afterwards I thought about it for a long time and I finally asked her how she'd known to do that.

"I don't know. I just did. I think I knew there was a little person in you who wanted to get out."

I was born in the spring of my thirtieth year and attended by her in loving kindness. She took me gently with her to where the darkness turns to sunlight.

Shirley is my good, dear friend. It wasn't long after, that my Aunt Ruth died.

There was a horrible dream that would come to me. . .haunt my nights, and terrify me. I don't remember exactly when it first came, but I was young. . .maybe six or seven the first time. . .and no matter how old I got, if it came back or even threatened to, I would do anything to keep from sleeping.

Sometimes it would stay away for several years only to re-emerge and grab the throat of my psyche again. Finally after having written some of the previous material I determined that if I could just write the dream down. . .capture it on paper. . .surely it would die. Like the bad witch in the Wizard of Oz it would simply shrivel up and go away in a cloud of steam.

I borrowed Shirley's cottage and took several days off. I was ready. Look out freedom. Here I come. Life can appear so simple from the vantage point of thirty-two.

I've told you about the little person so you will understand the dream and how it too had been inside me all this time. It's a nightmare with terrible power to come in to my consciousness at will. It is a fierce and beastly thing, and even though I am not a weak person, I still do not like to speak of it after all these years.

I am still afraid of it and will awaken cold and sweaty when it slips into my night. You should know that this dream is my madness or at least as close to madness as I want to get.

I have never liked to sleep. I will if I'm tired, but from the time I can remember, I've fought it. My mother used to catch me and hold me so close that I couldn't move any part of my body, and she would rock me in an old oak rocker in the living room until I'd fall asleep. I was always angry when I woke up. I felt betrayed.

When the dream comes, it lives in my head, and it has long connecting strings to various parts of my body. When it wants to, it can apply pressure on me by tightening the strings. I don't think about it a lot. It's just there.

When the dream catches me in my sleep, I go crazy and must fight my way back to being awake. If I can stay awake I am safer. . . not safe, just safer. I know the dream by heart and if I can stay awake it's as if I can see it coming and can run from it. If it catches me. . . . holds me tight so I can't get loose. . .even after I'm awake, the dream can make me lie in the darkness for hours, stiff with fear.

One of the dream's strings goes to my stomach and when it's tightened slightly it makes a dull, uncomfortable ache. Or it can pull so tightly that it makes me hold my stomach and double up into a ball and I lie on my side and try to fight it off by rocking myself. When it gets that bad I know it's just a matter of time before I'm exhausted and the dream will capture me.

Another string goes to my legs and makes them tense, wanting to run.

Still another goes down my arms and can turn my hands into fists, doubling them into tight knots which want to pound and strike out and I'm not really sure I can control them. They want to hit back.

There's one thick, tough string that loops around my chest and can cause me to nearly suffocate with silent screams. I can feel it move in my throat as it tightens and gags me.

Anyway, you need to understand that this dream I've had all my conscious life is inside me, alive right now, and I do not know if it can catch you in its strings. I only know it has me bound so tightly I cannot yet talk of it freely.

How long has it been since you fell out of bed? Since childhood? I still fall out so often it doesn't even wake my husband anymore when it happens. It's the dream that does it. It can push me, make me fall so I'm afraid of heights. Jim wakes up if I'm noisy, when the dream makes me jerk up and talk in my sleep and fight back....when I flail around trying to fight it off.

"Go back to sleep," he tells me. "You're alright." We've been married for years and he still doesn't know what the dream is about.

I've lived most of my life thinking things will get better in the future. But now I feel this pressure, this new tension growing in me, that the future is now and I have to face my fear of the dream fully if I'm to have any life left in which to be free. I have to beat this dream now or I never will. I'm going to try to cut its strings.

I don't know if I can do that.

I think the dream senses the coming fight and it flashes bits of itself in front of my consciousness and snaps the cord around my chest. It's like having previews to a movie shoved into your mind without warning and it makes my stomach jerk.

"What's the matter?" a friend said recently. She became concerned when she saw my eyes slam shut and my head jerk to one side. I do not like to think about the dream.

"Nothing," I said, trying to gain control of the emotion surging through me.

"Are you sure?"

"Yeah, I'm O.K."

But I'm not O.K.

It's funny. People think I'm fine. On the outside I write, chair committees in the community, raise a family, shop for food....lots of things. But inside where the strings can be drawn and the sleep seeps in on me, I'm not alright. Not yet anyway.

The dream would always enter my mind in the same way, like the curtain going up on act one. My mother is dead and laid out stiff and still at the funeral home I remember from my childhood. We're all there, my brother, my sisters, my dad. It's obviously nearing time to bury her. Music is playing. Old people, farm neighbors I've known all my life, some already dead, come shuffling in to pay their last respects. There's nothing for me to do in the dream except sit and watch. . .waiting for it to be over.

"She's dead," I start thinking. I don't feel anything as I sit there, except perhaps isolation from my family. They're all closed off, following my father's example. They sit like wooden statues in chairs made of flypaper. They do not move. They show no emotion and the organ music goes on and on.

I watch the old people come and go. It makes no sense that they are here. Many of them have been dead for years. They're harmless, I guess, but it is strange as I watch them slide silently past the casket. Where do they come from I wonder? Maybe old Dave Berg, the town mortician, never got around to burying them. Maybe he keeps them in a back room for additional guests on such occasions.

As the parade goes on to the tune of ceaseless music, the dream's loop around my chest begins to tighten. God! What if that's true? That thought seems to jump onto the floor and roll noisily around like a loose marble, causing a great commotion. People give me dirty looks and put their fingers to their lips. SSSSSh!

"Honestly! At her own mother's funeral!"

Why am I the only one who squirms? Look at my next of kin. They look at the casket and offer a few tears. I can't believe it. I have no tears to offer.

The strings in my body begin to strain against my self control and my legs and arms twitch.

"Sit still!" someone commands. I feel very young. I try to hang in, but it makes more sense to leave.

"Get up," I hear my silent voice urge. "Make yourself get up and go. Go before it's too late."

Just then my old school teacher comes in. I watch in fascination because she doesn't have a face. I recognize her by her shoes and the chalk dust on her dress. I wonder why she never did anything about what happened to me? Why didn't she call my Aunt Ruth? Instead she wrote "pneumonia" on my report card for the weeks I was absent from school after the worst beating. Pneumonia! A silent vote cast by a mouthless, non-seeing teacher who would not look at the truth. It makes sense that she should have no face now.

While I am watching her, old Dave the mortician, a ghost from my childhood, comes slipping up on me from the side and places himself in front of me with the exaggerated dignity that only funeral directors have. He presents me with a long box...like the ones roses come in...as if he were presenting a flag which had draped a coffin.

"You have to take care of these," he says in a tone which only the most insensitive could refuse. "Follow me," he says.

What do I do? I'm already squirming with discomfort and now I have this damned box. I look at my family and not one even glances in my direction. Silence. Yet others around me stare expectantly.

Dave has now moved to a side door and looks back with the impatience of a perturbed father. He adds an imploring jerk of his head for emphasis, and I rise reluctantly to follow.

I feel like I've wet my pants in public and everyone can see. I am sure they all know how I feel about her. I'm sure I'm going to be punished for my anger. There is no graceful way to exit. "Just get out of here," I tell myself. Just leave.

I follow the old man down a hallway and through a room full of empty caskets. I hate those places. Then we're in a different hallway and he stops in front of a large door.

"Here we are," he says as he sorts through a ring of keys.

"What's in here?" I ask about the box.

"We're here to make your mother happy," he says. "You'll know what to do," he says as he leaves me standing in front of an opened door. The box is beginning to feel heavy.

I step through the door and enter a bricked courtyard with a high board fence all around it. Above is a dull, overcast sky. A bird flies down and lands on the clothes lines which criss-cross the small area.

I become aware of what hangs from the lines just as the old man locks the door behind me. Hanging from the lines are dozens of pairs of limp arms, cut off at the shoulders, looking like so many damp towels hung by their corners. My god! Arms? Suddenly I'm acutely aware of the box I'm still holding. Oh, my god!

When I was a child I believed that if I could just wake up before the door was locked I'd be alright. If I could escape the sight of the arms it would only take me a few fearful nights to regain my self-control.

"Oh, god, no! Please don't make me do this", I'd beg. Over the years I tried everything. I dreamed of trying to kick in the door, climb the fence, screaming for help, or standing frozen for hours. But nothing helped once the door was locked. "Please, I would beg. . . . PPPPP-please." It's a very vicious dream.

Usually there was no escaping what was in the box. I'd put it down and remove the string that bound its cover and there was my mother's flesh. God, look! Her ring is still on her finger. I'd carry them to a place where there was room on the line to hang them, going past other arms, some old and soft with age, others no older than my own.

Taking all the courage I had, I'd try to place them on the line and this was the worst part of the dream. Sometimes if I hung the arms I could go to the door and it would be unlocked. Escape. It was one last bizarre act, one final, strange attempt to make her happy. When the dream ended like that I could simply feel it was over. . . . senseless, but over. The only question was, why me? Why did I have to have a dream like that? I would sometimes lie in bed for hours trying to figure that out.

But, in order to keep its power over me, the dream had another ending, too. Never let a kid know what to expect, right? Sometimes the arms on the lines became agitated and they would come to life. Suddenly they would grab my hair, start slapping me and shoving me hopelessly around. They could become overwhelmingly violent and beat me. Once they started there would be nothing I could do. There were too many of them.

"Let me go! Please! Le-le-let mmme go!" The worst was when it was my own mother's arms that started it or would grab me and hold me tight. Sometimes I would know it was coming because they would be flailing about before they were even out of the box. She would hold me while other hands reached for me. The only way she'd let me go was if I said "I'm sorry." I don't know why but if I felt sorrow for some unknown, incomprehensible act, I might get loose from her. Maybe.

Sometimes I would scream and fight the arms with all my might. Let me go! Let me go! But that might only make things worse when I was a child because I might wake someone up and they would come and touch me.

"Wake up," my mother would say. "Wake up!" She'd try to shake me awake.

"Let me go! Let me go!" I'd scream. My god it's real. She's got me. "Let me go!"

I would hit at her and she'd shake me some more. "No! No! No! No!" I'd scream.

"She's crazy wild," I'd hear her tell my father.   "No! No! No! NO!" Fight her. I'd scream until I was crazy. I'd fight for fear the arms would tear me apart. They would destroy me. Get loose! Try to get loose! "NO!NO! NO! Let me go! Let me go!"

She would try to hold me down on the bed. "Let me go! Let me go!"

During those long, crazy exhausting bouts the real terror would set in. . . . I could no longer tell the dream from her.

"Leave me alone," I'd beg her. "Don't touch me. P-P-Please don't touch me. Please. . . ."

"Alright, if you'll stay on your bed."

"Don't touch me!" Long after she was gone I'd lie there whispering to the gods, begging them. . . "Please don't let her get me. . . . please!" And I would not sleep. Sleep was one enemy I could beat sometimes.   "Aunt Ruth. . . . please, Aunt Ruth. Please come get me," I'd think.

But I'm grown now and I think I understand more. The punch

line of the dream is simple. My mother will have the power to destroy me even after she's dead and no one will stop her even then.

Well, now I will stop you, dream. My friends, the ones who love me and give me kind words and who have gentle arms and hands...they will stop you. When I'm torn open with pain and most vulnerable, I will tell other people, so I won't get caught there alone. I will not take that box from the old mortician again. Who in the hell is he to tell me I have to make her happy? Shit. I will make me happy. I will treat my mother with decency, but I will not be responsible for her happiness and no one's going to make me responsible for it either. This is my life, too.

If you come for me tonight, dream, I will use a new weapon on you...strong new thoughts that will kill you if you're not already dead. The words are...

"My mother cannot make me crazy". Hear me well. The words are not "MMy mmmother cannot make mme crazy."

This is no mere pillow wrapped around the head of my childness to fend you off. This is a weapon, a sword, and I will kill you, dream. I will. Do not come for me tonight. My mother cannot make me crazy....not now or ever.

I felt a rush of victory at getting the dream on paper. I was winning. Finally.

My life was better - especially with friends who cared and were supportive. I felt I was entering a new period of living when the old feelings and burden would be gone or at least have receded far enough into the background for me to put my energy elsewhere. I did well for several years. And I slept well, even if naively. I really began to believe it was all over.

BOOK TWO

The following material was written about 5 years later, after there was a drastic turn of events in my life. I'd managed to wire together a good support system, I'd moved the dream away from the power base it had had in my child's mind, and I felt more resolved about the physical and verbal abuse I'd experienced. The little person part of me had more emotional control and my life was steadier and calm. And I had a tremendous desire to move on and put it all behind me. I felt good and productive in my work running the substance abuse program at the local tribal center, and to a large extent, felt I'd reclaimed my life.

Let it go. That became the new method. "Look," I remember saying to Shirley "I can't go on dragging this thing around forever. I think the only thing to do is cut it loose and go on. So life wasn't exactly what I would have chosen. Maybe that's tough. Too bad. There isn't really anything I can do about it now. I guess you just put it behind you and live your life or there's never any life that you live where (the abuse) is not the agenda."

So, I did. I thought less about my childhood and lived more in the here and now. I worked, taught, wrote, made friends, traveled, learned a lot and survived. My kids grew up and my marriage grew apart but I was making it. And from my perspective, the past ten years have been the most successful and together of my life.

"It's done, I guess," I remember saying. "It's over." After I wrote down the dream we drank wine and talked for a long time.

I felt strongly that I could go on from here. Why not? I'm a strong person with lots of support. Weren't my friends being supportive? Hadn't I developed the skills needed to write this thing through?

I should be thankful. I'm bright and creative and will find my way. Hadn't I figured out to copy all those pictures of myself as a child? And I looked at them, to see in them the truth. I had learned that there was this little kid in me and that I needed to take better care of her and help her grow and heal. "Who could do it better? I told my friends. If I am ever to be free it will be because I free myself and I think the writing is the way out.

And that's how it happened. I wrote it all down and put it away. Free at last and all that jazz. Neatness counts. It was gone.

But things began to come unwired for me in my late thirties. And I had no idea how difficult life would get.

Tunk.

It was such a small explosion. Only the sound of a newspaper thrown against the front door on an October Saturday morning. Tunk.

I had been at a traditional feast the night before — a naming ceremony for the son of Robert, a close friend and co-worker and his wife Sherri. It is an important ceremony in Indian culture in which a child is given an Indian name. By participating you are more in touch with your own spirit and the spirits of others in the circle. It leaves you calmed and centered. You cannot be in the presence of a pipe without feeling these things.

Tunk.

We had driven home in the cold briskness of the starry fall night and I'd felt strengthened. The pipe ceremony had helped me feel part of something bigger than myself.

Tunk. The sun was shining. I walked out on the porch and took joy in the beauty of the day.

I picked up the paper while looking at the pretty leaves. I like fall. Tunk. Such a small explosion.

Headline: "AGGIE SULTITZ DIES, THE CARING COMMISSIONER"

The words shoved a howling chain saw into my stomach. "Ah..Ah..Ahhh," is what I kept screaming inside. "AGGIEEE" is what I was trying to say.

I'd never felt it before. My god. Nothing had ever torn me open and ripped my soul like that moment. Aggie was one of my closest friends.

The phone began to ring shortly after that. People calling . . . saying stuff. "I'm so sorry." "What happened?" "Did you know?"

The eulogy, I thought! Aggie had asked me to do her eulogy about two years ago. "ah..Ah..Ahh.."

"I know how close you were to Mama. She loved you a lot, Kathy." Aggie's family wanted me to be with them. Her daughters wanted me to hold their babies.

Going down that aisle... following the casket... I only remember Dan and Shirley being with me and Dan's arm around my shoulder. And Clemma stepping close to hug me.

Candles, music, prayers and priests. Sitting up in the front of a mass of people and cameras.

"God has taken a loved one from us. . ."

I looked out at the faces and saw a pew full of Native women who made me think of a party we'd had at Aggie's boat only two months before.

"We can not know why she was taken. . ."

Just get it over with, I remember thinking.

Then it was my turn.

"My name is Kathy Evert and I speak to you today because Aggie asked me to. . ."

"Ah...Ah..." Just hang on.

Going back down the aisle... going to the grave.

"That was beautiful, Kathy. You said what a lot of us felt."

"I know how much you loved her."

"AHHHH..." I didn't cry or get unglued. I think a lot of people were amazed at how together I was that day.

"I don't know how you did that. God, you're strong." "ah..."

There was a voice inside me which kept making the same sound over and over, but it never came out. I kept thinking somehow it would and the pain would be eased.

Tunk.

Sweat. Heart pounding. 2:30 A.M. Awake again.

Night after night the same thing happens — sleep for a couple of hours and then jerk awake to be followed by hours of silence and panic.

Lie still, I'd say to myself. Maybe you'll go back to sleep.

But I would not sleep. Fragments of memory, pieces of emotion would begin to float in front of my mind. . . like some emotional kaleidoscope of things to avoid. I saw them all a thousand times. Twisting surges of emotion would travel through my abdomen. More and more I'd have to think . . ."Do you really want to live like this? What's the point?" I thought a lot about suicide.

It was 7:30 AM. Just dial the phone, I thought.

"Ellen?"

"Kathy? Is this Kathy?"

Stay calm, I thought. But it was no use. I put my hand over the receiver and threw up in the kitchen sink.

"What's wrong?"

"I'm not making it," I said.

"Yes you are. You're alright."

Panic. Hang up, you fool. Get yourself under control. But my voice kept talking.

"I'm not alright." I struggled. "I..I..IIII'm not making it." Calm down. Breathe slower.

"Where are you?" said Ellen. "Can you come here? Can you get here? Come on. Just put on a coat and come."

By the time I got there I was feeling like a fool and explaining that I was simply too tired.

"Sue?"

"Hi. How ya doing?"

"I've been better. Listen, do you have some time this weekend to talk some things through with me? I need to get a handle on all this stuff that's going on."

"Sure. You probably need to just process it. There's been a lot lately, hasn't there?"

"Yeah. Too much."

"I can hear it in your voice."

We had dinner out and then talked in her apartment for hours. After a long time she said, "Look, it's normal that you should feel depressed." "I'm not depressed. I just don't like dealing with all this at once."

"Listen fucker," she said, launching into the kind of verbal barrage only old friends can, "You're depressed. You may not want to look at that, and you may be doing a hell of a job covering it up to everybody, but you're depressed. It's time to see somebody."

Part of me fought against those words and part of me caved in, all at the same time.

"I guess that's why I wanted to talk to you." I said slowly. "I guess I respect your professional judgement, and in all honesty I think I really don't know what to do on the other side of the fence. I feel stupid. I put people into treatment all the time and I really don't know what to do now."

So she gave me a name and I called on Monday. But by the time I got to him I'd sunk deeper into my own emotional swamp. And the same question — do you really want to go on like this? — was in my face again only shorter — Do you really want to live?

So I talked to him. It wasn't a very emotional. experience. I just laid it out. This happened, that happened and I feel like this. Period. It was like eating a mayonnaise sandwich on white bread. No big deal.

Boom. I'm awake. 1:30 A.M. Suddenly I'm aware of my chest feeling tight and my heart racing. I think about getting up and I can't do it. Why don't I just go downstairs and read, I think. But I don't do it. The longer I lay there, the longer I have the feeling I'm lying next to a dark hole and I'm slowly going to slide into it. I wrap myself around a sweater that was Aggie's and I feel like Linus in the comic strips with his blanket. But at least I don't dream.

During all this my mother became ill, was getting physically worse, and was in the hospital. I visited often and my parents expected me to always be on hand to keep track of and interpret the medical developments. But the visits — being alone with my mother — were often agony.

Driving home from the hospital, more than once, I'd pound the steering wheel and keep yelling "I know...I know...I kno..kno..know." Part of me consciously thought "Know what?" I tried to think rationally about my feelings...tried to deal with them...but every time I'd leave the hospital....every time I'd escape from being caught in that small space with my past...I couldn't talk. I'd drive around trying to calm down before I'd go home or back to the office. I'd have to struggle to get my breathing under control before I could go back to the other space where I felt confident and under control. I learned that people don't necessarily change and get kinder just because they're dying.

She had an operation to try to find out what was wrong with her stomach. The surgery started at 10:00 so I waited until after lunch to go to the hospital.

My dad and oldest sister were waiting in the lobby. They didn't want to miss the doctor so they'd not gone for lunch and dad was getting a headache from not eating. I scouted around and found a vending machine.

"You haven't heard anything yet?" I asked.

"No," Anna said with an exaggerated sigh. "They just leave you waiting. They've probably gone to lunch."

I went to the desk to find out if she was in the recovery room yet. No.

God that's maybe three and a half hours of surgery! I thought.

We waited. My sister read a book and Dad looked uptight. I opened my mail from the office and got bored. My aunt showed up, also very tense. Pretty soon it was four and a half hours. No doctor. The woman at the desk now said my mother was in the recovery room, but still no doctor.

"Let me go call Jim," I said.

My cousin Jim is my mother's doctor. When he finally got on the phone he sounded very uptight.

"It's not good," he said. "It's cancer and very widespread. What we thought was an ulcer has grown very fast and there's not much we really can do. We can take care of the pain. . . we can make her more comfortable. . . but .. it's not good."

There was a little more technical description. . . some medical stuff. . . but that was about it.

"It will go very fast," he said with his voice trailing off.

"How fast?"

"A few months. . . it's hard to say."

"God," I said as my stomach tightened. I looked and saw my father listening to my end of the conversation.

"I'm sorry," said Jim.

"Yeah..yeah," I said and hung up. I knew I had to tell my dad.

I heard my voice talking, comforting, my arms were around him as we walked back to where the others were. . . I was the strong one again. Calm. Calm and strong. That was me.

("AAh. . .Aah. . . .")

Later I told my brother and other sister. I held my dad while he cried. And the next day as the family grimly gathered I helped people talk about what was happening.

That afternoon my mother woke up and asked me to help her do something. When I leaned near her she grabbed my hands and held on with surprising strength.

"What's wrong with me?" she asked.

"It's not good," I echoed Jim. Maybe he knows how to say it.

"Is it cancer?"

"I'm not going to lie to you."

"How bad is it?"

"You're in for a tough fight."

It felt like all the other volume in the world had been turned off except for this one small conversation. I knew it really hadn't, however, because when it was over my sister was still talking about a cake recipe. I felt a little strange. Why was I responding this way?

43

Why did my mother ask me and why wasn't I talking about apple-sauce cake recipes like the others? Why the hell do I get so involved?

I work as a supervisor in a low budget substance abuse agency and when I got back to the office that afternoon, I was met by two homicide detectives who were flashing their badges. One of my clients was a prime suspect in a murder and had told the police he was with me at the time of the shooting. Would you believe it! Seven thirty on a Saturday morning?

"Sorry. I can't talk without a court order. But were you with him?"

"Man, I can't tell you that. The laws regarding substance abuse files are stricter than for any other. Get me some paper and we'll talk."

He smiled just slightly, "Are you married?"

"Fucker", I thought. I knew what he was thinking and he knew I knew.

"Yes, but I sleep with my clients." I smiled sweetly. "You want information, go to court." He made me mad.

The next day my client's sister came in. "He never had a gun before, but I saw one out at the cottage last week. There were two boxes of bullets. When I heard the news about who was killed I thought immediately about my brother."

"My god", I thought. You're the one he really hates. He's told me so over and over. But you don't know it, do you?

"Uh....I don't want to alarm you, but....you should be cautious....don't be frightened....just"

My heart was about to explode.

"Yes, I think you should talk to the police when they come over this afternoon." My voice was calm and reassuring as she left.

I called the damned detective. "Get that paper as fast as you can..."

That night it seemed almost a haven to go to the hospital after work. My mother seemed upset. So much for havens.

"I'm sorry," she said.

"About what?"

"About what happened."

I truly didn't know what she was talking about. "You can't help it if you're sick." She just cried. I didn't know what to say or do.

A nurse came in and told her she had to get up and walk a little. She was very weak and needed help. As she got to her feet she put her arms around me and held on.

"I'm sorry," she said again. "It should never have happened."

Suddenly her meaning fell into place. "Oh Jesus", I thought. Not that, too. Suddenly I was falling backwards into my childhood....it was back to the woodpile....whop....please, don't....please don't....Boom! It was a huge explosion.

Hang on, I kept thinking. I yelled in the car all the way home. I spent hours talking to the police during the next two days. I called Ellen and a few days later Sue. My client killed himself and in all honesty I have to say I was relieved.

When I went to see the counsellor Sue had recommended, I'd felt a million miles from him. I couldn't reach him....I couldn't make it across. I was going down.

My mother would sometimes just cry when she looked at me. She had four more hours of surgery and eleven pints of blood plus four more units every night for a week. She kept spitting up blood.

My client's sister went over the edge at the funeral. I dreamed the dream again.

Finally the phone rang.

"Hello, Kathy? This is Geri. How are you doing?"

"Let me get on another phone if you really want to know."

We talked and I had the sense of someone calm listening.

"And I don't know," I told her. "How do you find somebody and how do you know if you need to go into therapy?"

Geri is a gutsy woman who's dealt with a lot of life head on. She made sense.

She talked about what she thought she saw happening with me and how things were piling up on me. I told her I'd gone to see the counsellor Sue had mentioned and it just didn't work.

"He's a nice guy," I said, "but maybe that's not what I need.

Maybe I just need to hang in.''

But some friends are secure enough to tell you when you're full of crap.

"And all your losses that you're feeling right now are with women. Shirley. Aggie. Your mother.'' She continued. She knew. Finally someone could hear. "You need to see a woman and you need to see someone who can help with the dream. Someone who won't be afraid to hold you and let you be little again.''

"I don't want to be little again.''

"You probably have to if there's going to be the kind of deep healing you need.''

I think the two things that made the difference. . . .that helped me try one more time. . . .were her calm voice and the words "deep healing''. Well, and the dream, and no sleep and the question — Do you really want to live? — which kept being asked in my head. I'm grateful that Geri called.

I called the name Geri gave me and made an appointment. When I got there I was very brave.

"Hi. I'm Kathy Evert.'' I shook her hand. I stood tall. I took the "Well, here we are — both mature and professional'' approach.

I told her I appreciated that she'd agreed to see me for more than one hour because I felt I needed to talk this all through. It was just that life was a bit much at the moment and I needed to sit down, talk about it and get on with things. (I was going for a one shot, very fast resolution.) So she asked me to tell her about myself and what seemed to be the problem. Eventually I got to my usual routine about having been abused as a child.

"But I think that's pretty much under control now,'' I told her. Yet as I said it I caught myself with a doubled up fist, slowly and lightly beating the arm of the chair, and I carefully relaxed my hand and hoped she hadn't seen that little gesture. She showed nothing in her face, but I was to learn with time that I'd met my match. She missed nothing.

By the end of the first session, "my kid'' — the eskimo child who'd floated away on the ice — came back with amazing impact. I felt tension in my legs and Inie encouraged me to "stay with that'' and it grew until my whole body shook.

"What was that?" I said afterwards.

"I think maybe it was your body remembering how it felt to be beaten," she said calmly. "I think maybe we'll need to talk about that more."

Talk we did for over three hours and somehow before it was over I had an irresistible urge to sit on the floor in front of her and put my head in her lap.

"What's happening?" she asked about my obvious discomfort at the idea. After realizing the thought wouldn't just go away, I told her.

"That's O.K." she said calmly.

It wasn't O.K., for crying out loud. I was nearly forty years old and I'd just met this woman.

But the kid in me did it and I cried and cried. Then Inie leaned forward, took my head between her hands, and spoke very softly in my ear.

"It's alright," she said in almost a whisper. "It's alright to look at these things and to talk about what happened. They've been taboo all this time but it's safe to talk about them here. You can tell me."

I think for the first time someone talked directly to the kid. The adult me was shaken but the kid loved it. The kid wanted more.

I hated going back. I hated the flood of relentless memories which began to emerge from within me. And that's how it happened. I began a lengthy process of week after week taking a young, hurt, needy part of me to treatment.

As time passed, there was a tremendous bond formed between the three of us — Inie, the adult me, and "the kid" as the little person became known. But I never learned to like it. I hated going to therapy.

"What does she look like?" Shirley asked.

"I don't know."

"What do you mean, you don't know? You were with her for hours. Didn't you look at her?"

"Some."

"Is she short, tall, young, what?"

"I think she's taller than I am and she's older than I am." Shirley was making me uncomfortable. It had been all I could do to go talk to Inie, let alone remember what she looked like. In truth, after several hours with her, I might not have been able to pick her out in a small group.

I think I didn't have a clearer image of Inie because the sessions were very physical. And for a long time I had no idea where these physical reactions were coming from.

Looking back I know I was taking the kid to treatment but early on I had no awareness of that. Often I would talk with Inie for twenty minutes or so and I would feel tension growing — usually in my stomach, arms and legs. And it seemed like sooner or later she'd ask something like "What's happening in your stomach?" and it would be like she pulled a trigger.

My jaw would tighten and I'd feel my neck muscles begin to bang my head against the back of the chair. I'd feel Inie put her hands in a position to protect my head from the banging, I'd make the "Ah, ah, ah," sound, and I'd feel my whole body shake and slam around. Tears would pour down my cheeks. That's what I'd remember. It would be like an emotional/physical eruption and I — the adult me at least — would get lost somewhere.

Later I'd wake up on the floor and sort of "come back" to the room and Inie. My arms and legs were often heavy and tired, my face wet with tears, and I'd have no idea of the time. Inie says it was not hypnosis and I believe her. Whatever it was I think she was pretty gutsy to allow it to happen week after week and I think now it was the kid in me releasing screaming, flailing, howling rage about the abuse she'd experienced. But in the

beginning I thought I was going mad. "We have to trust the process,"
Inie would say. And afterwards I'd always have this feeling that some-
thing important had happened or been re-experienced but it was as if
it had occurred on the other side of lace curtains. As if the real meat
of the session had been so close but was obscured from the adult me.
And I would feel as if I had been very far away, and often was exhausted.
"What happened?" Inie would ask.
I usually wasn't sure. I'd be left more with feelings than with answers
or clear images. As time went on we got better at talking these outbursts
through.

How do you relate that there's this other part of yourself and
that your own body feels what the other part remembers even
if the adult you doesn't have a conscious awareness of it? I don't
know how to adequately express my discomfort at all that. "Trust
the kid," Inie says. "Let her tell you." To feel there is another
person alive and active within my mind and body is not exactly
my idea of a good time.

It's hard to go. It's hard to take off my coat like I'm going to
stay. It's hard to sit down. It's hard to talk and to look at her.
Fear wells up in me when I get in touch with unfamiliar feelings
and thoughts.

And it's not as if there's any agreement between the adult me
and this other part. It's like a war at times. For one thing the
kid has almost no emotional control. Fear is raw and wild. And
once it gets away from me neither I nor the kid can get it under
control easily. As an experience it can quickly go from uncomfortableness to terror to feeling foolish afterwards.

"You're really afraid of me aren't you?" Inie asked at one point.
She'd moved her hand toward me and I'd stiffened.

"No," I said and part of me meant it. The adult me had no
reason to be afraid of her and, in fact, had a lot of trust in her.

But the kid is scared. The kid doesn't want to be touched by
anybody. The kid makes my body taut and withdrawn.

Later I thought, "I must be crazy. Why would I react like that? She must think I'm off the wall."

The first time with Inie I told her about the worst beating and the emotions sort of swallowed me up. My legs hurt terribly for a while. For days after that my legs felt different, looser and freer.

Then on Thanksgiving Day my mother reached out and touched my coat collar as I was leaving her house and it set off a flood in me. By the time I got home I couldn't sit still and had to go for a long walk. Walk. Walk. Faster. It was as if maybe I could outwalk my feelings. I walked all weekend. On Sunday night I called Inie's house.

When we finally got together that week I was scared. I wanted her to see the scars on my back. I wanted her to touch my back. And I didn't really know why. Maybe to know someone knows what happened to me. "This is crazy," I thought, and I gave myself my wisest counsel. "You're crazy." But something got me back into her little office.

The third time I took her some writing and some pictures of me when I was a child. I'm not sure why.

"Does it really do any good," I thought? "Why dig around in all that old crap. It's done. It's over. Let it go." I hated therapy.

One night very early in this process I awoke feeling for all the world like someone had been picking me up — lifting me out of bed — and my heart was pounding. I knew it was crazy. Someone would have been very large and strong to pick me up like that — as if I were a child. And then I remembered something I hadn't thought of in years.

For some reason my mother was into giving me enemas. She would get me out of bed in the middle of the night and take me into the kitchen and lay me on the counter by the sink. I can still remember the moonlight coming in the window.

She always told me I needed to be cleaned out and I never understood what she meant by that.

We had no indoor bathroom and our water came from a hand pump at the kitchen sink. Over to the right from where she put me on the counter was a big old wood cook stove and I also remember the lid being off part of it and the fire and coals inside made an orange glow in the room. Sometimes she'd put a metal poker in the fire or coals and when it was removed it would be red with heat. I still remember very clearly the shape of it in the darkness.

I know I wasn't very old because my parents still live in the same house and looking at that counter I know I was a very small body then. Above where she'd put me was a knife rack and the rack is different but the knife I remember still hangs there.

She would fill the enema bag with cold water from the pump and tell me over and over again to be quiet. Silence was the one absolute rule.

She would put her fingers in my vagina and insert the enema tube in my rectum and tell me I needed to be cleaned out. I didn't understand and it hurt. She wasn't gentle in the way she touched me.

If I cried she would demand silence. If I continued to make noise she would take down a knife and place it on my chest. She would put my nightie up around my neck and lay the knife on my bare skin. The memory of how it felt is still very real.

"Be quiet," she'd demand. "Keep your mouth shut." I would be terrified and the way I'd keep from screaming was to shove a wad of my clothing into my mouth.

"Be quiet." Over and over silence was the rule.

I told Inie about it and it was difficult — humiliating to talk about it. But at the same time it was a relief too.

"It's good you can finally talk about it," she said.

My comfort with Inie was growing with each meeting, which was an even bigger relief. But our work together began to make other things happen in me.

Another image floated to the surface of my consciousness. I began to see myself as a small child, maybe three or so, crouched in the corner of my parents bedroom. I looked frightened, sad, and cornered.

As my depression rolled on, I would sometimes lie on my bed and watch a mental parade of images and thoughts go by for the thousandth time. I would see that little frightened face over and over and then it occurred to me I could not have seen myself like that. I would instead have been looking at something else. What?

And then as if a TV camera, my mind seemed to turn around and I saw my mother lying in bed with her arms reaching out to me. That's all. But in that moment I knew the problem, that all my uproar from my childhood was not just because of physical abuse. I could feel my mother's hands on me and in me.

The images stopped floating past my mind. It felt like the silence after an enormous explosion. Things were falling out of the air and into place . . . crashing around me in a new order and making a different kind of sense. For the first time when I thought of the physical abuse I didn't ask myself why it had happened as much as face the possibility that maybe she really did want to kill me to shut me up. I had always felt like the family skeleton and maybe I really am in a much deeper sense than I ever realized.

It makes my legs ache to think about it. I don't know how I feel, sort of numb inside but I also feel used or something. I can't really focus on it and I'm not sure I want to. Do I really want to know any more than I do? I now remember it happened. Isn't that enough?

"Lie still," she'd say.

She would insert the end of the hose in me and my insides would flood with cold water. It hurt. I can still feel it. I could feel it creeping deeper and higher into my body and it would make me shiver with cold.

"Hold it in," she'd demand, sometimes holding my buttocks together. "Hold it in," was the second absolute rule. When I wouldn't or couldn't, she would do it all over again.

Be quiet. Lie still. Hold it in. And there was the knife. Cold and hard it felt like an ice mountain on my chest. The tip of it would nearly touch my throat and my chest would feel paralyzed. I'd always end up with my mouth full of clothes.

Part of me doesn't want to know any more. Part of me, right now as I type, feels tight in my chest and feels my heart beating faster. That part of me feels fear at exposing this, and guilt, and says "Be rational. It's gone. You understand it. Leave it alone. Be careful."

But the kid feels differently. The kid told in the first place and wants to run to Inie and tell her, to be held, and protected.

But protected from what? The past? It is gone. It is over. I'd just like it to get back into the box and leave me alone.

Driving back in the car from an out of town visit, I thought I'd suffocate. The day before, on Sunday afternoon, my chest had gotten tight. At first I thought I was getting a cold. But as the tightness grew I knew it wasn't a cold. It was the knife. It felt as if it was there on my chest again.

"Pick it up," I told myself. "Pick it up and take it off."

I moved my hand as if to do that and I thought, what if I can't deal with it? What if I get angry? What if I hurt someone? I thought about my mother and could feel the tension growing in me but at the same time I realized I was holding an imaginary knife over my own body. My god, I thought. What if I hurt myself? And I put the knife back.

By the time I got to Inie that week I felt like the weight of the knife would crush my lungs and chest.

"I don't like myself," I told her. "I feel embarrassed that I don't have the strength to deal with this whole thing myself. That may be wrong, not a healthy attitude, but I have survived and kept what self respect I do have by taking care of myself. I don't know how to be when I can't do that. It's not even a real knife. It's the black bear in the path the elders talk about. What do you do if the bear blocks your way?"

Anyway, we struggled with it. It must have been at least an hour of sweat and labored breathing but I could not take it off by my own hand. I asked Inie to take it. She wouldn't do that and I could not make it go away. The adult me was stuck deep inside the kid's fears and terror. I eventually couldn't talk.

"You're not supposed to make a sound, are you?" Inie finally said. "You're not supposed to make a sound but now you're about to, aren't you? You're about to scream, aren't you?"

And, pulled along by some invisible psychic threads, I went over the edge. Up out of my insides came a terrible, agonized sound. I'd never heard my voice scream like that.

"Yes, scream. She'll have to move the knife now. People are coming now. They'll help you. You're not alone."

I couldn't stop screaming.

For a brief moment I felt suspended in some kind of psychological mid-air. I clung to Inie like she was life itself. She had her arms around me and when I finally stopped screaming, she sort of squeezed that last bit of breath out of me.

"Good. It's good you screamed. You made her move the knife. Now she'll have to take it away."

I heard it all. I understand it. I know there can be real benefits from tearing loose an old piece of pain like that. But why does my heart pound harder when I think about it? If it's done, if that piece is over, are we done? Is the therapy over? Or was it simply the cork in the bottle? It scares me. Maybe at the bottom I'm really afraid to trust Inie that much. Maybe the kid and I aren't really that far apart when we get right down to the bottom and both of us want to say "Please be careful with me."

Even after all this, my focus was on the fact that my mother had done a lot of crazy things with me. But I struggled to keep the full meaning of the sexualness of all this from crashing through on me. I held out as long as I could. Then the kid got into the act and forced me to begin to accept that it was more than just physical abuse. I'd gotten stuck on the pain of realizing that maybe my mother had really tried to kill me to keep me from ever telling about the craziness of the enemas, the knife, etc.

One pale winter morning the kid said, "I want to tell you something." Inie leaned forward and I whispered in her ear, and I/the kid snitched on all the big people from my childhood.

"Sometimes it feels like something is probing at my rectum."

"Yeah?" She listened. Her arms were around me and I felt safe.

"I just wanted to tell you that. I don't like it."

"Do you want to talk about it?"

I shook my head no. I felt about nine. "I just wanted to tell you."

"It's good you did," she said calmly. "We'll talk about it when you're ready — when you want to."

It was at the end of the time with Inie that day and it felt like there were three people in the conversation.

The kid felt safe, relieved, secure and satisfied when she left. But the adult me was uneasy because even before the word probing was out of my mouth I knew the kid was spilling the beans on something. There were two parts of me and the adult had no conscious awareness of having been sexually abused. There was a connection with the word probing and the enemas, but the enemas seemed so bizarre that I didn't understand them, much less think about them.

And then there was Inie — always willing to let the therapy take its own course and to hear anything the kid wanted to say. Very early on it was clear that Inie loved the kid. "It's good you told me," she said.

There was a relentlessness to what emerged in the sessions, and the next week it was like the kid brought it up again. Somehow it felt like things were breaking loose.

"We have to trust the process," Inie always says.

Trust.

Keep trusting, I tell myself. Don't panic. Don't run. And as calmly as possible I keep myself here — in process — and realize that maybe its the sound of my own voice screaming which feels like things breaking around me.

We had a long conversation about trust and cultural differences and I inched a little closer to Inie emotionally.

"A couple weeks ago I met with a young woman from Planned Parenthood. We were working toward setting up some groups at the Tribal Council and she was telling me what was available in the community to deal with various aspects of sexuality. For some reason I asked her what was around for victims of incest."

I really don't know what she answered. Something about a support group, I think.

"I could hardly sit in my chair," I told Inie.

In truth I could hardly stay in my skin.

"And she just went on talking, but I was really uncomfortable."

"It set off a volcano in you?"

"Yeah. (Keep trusting.) I want . . . . (inch by painful inch) . . . . I want to talk about that someday. Not now. But someday I want to talk about it. (Trust. Trust.) I can still feel it."

"The probing?"

I could only shake my head yes. I'd gone as far as I could go.

"We'll deal with that. When you're ready."

"Not now."

"No. When you're ready."

Ready. Ready. When you're ready. It's never just "forget it". It's always "When you're ready, trust the process/when you're ready process."

God I hated it. It was like some other uncontrollable part of me would go veering off in that direction no matter how much the other part of me resisted.

The last thing Inie said to me that day was "Well, you have my number. Call if you need to talk." Very calm. Very relaxed.

It was a Thursday forenoon — New Year's Eve — and 1982 was upon me — stark and real — a year of reckoning. By Saturday at 9:00 AM I was in agony. My night had been filled with horrible images/memories of a sexually brutal past. I had not slept and my vagina, rectum and dignity were all in pain. I called Inie. Thank god she at least was calm.

Within an hour in Inie's little room, the reality that my mother had abused me not only physically but sexually, fell on me like a giant redwood. And the force of it falling shook my world and everything in it.

Within twenty-four hours the adult me had struggled to put every fragment of memory that had surfaced onto paper and taken it and put it in Inie's mail box. It was like writing "return to sender" on my own consciousness. I tried to send those thoughts/ideas away. I could not sleep with them in the house.

I remember. It keeps coming and I remember — ready or not. It sounds like breaking glass — like being somewhere where there are thousands of windows being broken. They are crashing around me and I know it's going to keep happening. Something is out to smash every window, mirror and piece of glass in this place. It's frightening, but I also sense as it goes on that I am not breaking. I am not what's building up under foot and crunches when I walk.

Within forty-eight hours there was so much glass I couldn't hear myself think.

Ben. I never really liked him. He's my mother's cousin. He always brought alcohol. Beer. In brown bottles. . . . in boxes. . . . in excess. He and his Mississippi born wife, Rose, would come for weekends to pick strawberries or go fishing.

She would call me "skeeter", a country word for mosquito, because I was so skinny. But in the summers she would focus on something else.

"There's the pickaninny," she'd say. And I remember her saying, "That child will look like a nigger by the time school starts."

But Ben was the real problem. I know now he was an alcoholic, but then I didn't understand. Neither of my parents drank much at other times. but they did with him. Things changed when Ben and Rose came. It was a mixed bag. We were so poor and isolated that any company was a big event and they would sometimes bring treats or foods we didn't get otherwise. But the uncomfortableness of seeing my parents change was the other side of the coin. Things were not very secure when they came.

Ben talked dirtier than anyone I've ever known. I know words are just words, but the continuing focus on the crudest descriptions of sex through jokes and blunt statements and by talking about the people around him was probably overwhelming. No one else I knew in that little world talked like that and I think I was shocked to see my parents accept it in him.

Once I came into the house and they were all playing cards.

"Watch this," Ben told them. "Come here, Katie, and see these cards."

As I went to him he said I had to sit on his lap to see them. So

I sat on his lap and they all laughed at the expression on my face when I looked at the cards.

"What are they doing? Huh?"

They were regular playing cards, but instead of the usual markings they had very graphic photos of men and women doing various sex acts including things like beer bottles in women's vaginas. I got terribly embarrassed and tried to leave but he held me on his lap. Through his pants I could feel his penis get hard and he would move me to rub me against it. Somehow the card game and drinking just went on, and the pictures passed before my eyes and he pressed against my bottom. Neither of my parents showed concern.

I remember. When I spoke to Inie Thursday about the incest, I felt some uneasy discomfort. But as soon as I said it, as soon as it reached the light of day and consciousness, it exploded. Vague discomfort became real physical pain in my vagina and rectum. The narrow focus of remembering enemas and my mother has expanded in a new kaleidoscope of images and words which I can't turn off. I remember. Glass is crashing everywhere.

I remember being very tiny and being rubbed against a male penis. I don't remember who it was or where it happened. I can also feel being held across my chest and thighs with a penis between my legs — inserted from behind. I can feel the warmth of the person's body and the ejaculation and the semen on my body.

I remember Ben tickling me. He would do it for a long time until I could hardly breath. My mother would tell me to settle down after it went on a while and Ben would put me on his lap and tell me to sit there until I calmed down. But he'd continue to tickle me enough to keep me wiggling and I would feel his penis pointed into my rectum. My mother would always blame me for the commotion.

I remember being awake in a crib in my parent's bedroom while they had sex. I could hear the noises and sometimes see them in the dim light. I slept in their room until I was about five.

I can see Ben with his penis exposed near the outside toilet we had. He wasn't going to the bathroom and was standing there looking at me. To remember it makes me feel like running.

I remember seeing my oldest sister coming from the barnyard crying and holding herself. I asked her what was wrong and she just kept going towards the house. I remember feeling something was very wrong. I also remember her talking very emotionally to my mother in the kitchen one time. She said something like "No wonder he's like that. She never wears any underpants." It was often quite clear, especially in the summer, that Rose didn't wear underpants.

And I can feel him inside me. It hurts. I don't know any more than that, but it's him I feel. He's big and heavy and the message is very familiar. "Lie still and be quiet." He smells like beer. I can't make myself scream. I can hardly breathe and the muscles in my throat are jerking.

I think of my mother telling me I wasn't clean. That she had to make me clean. Shit. Why didn't she just protect me? I also see the image of her with her arms coaxing me into bed. I don't want to know what that means. I know what I feel and what I saw in my mind — the child shrinking into a corner — and that's enough. No more. No more. No more. Inside me there's a child's voice screaming, "Don't touch me! Leave me alone!"

The new kaleidoscope began during the day after I told Inie I wanted to talk about incest. That night I kept waking up wet with tears and not knowing what I had been dreaming. The tears scared me. For all the pain of this fall and the therapy, there have been few tears.

The following morning the images kept passing through my head and I couldn't make them go away. There was pressure and pain pulsing in my rectum and terrible twisting surges which began in my vagina and passed through my abdomen. I tried to do things to make it go away but I was having real trouble keeping my emotional balance.

Trust. Trust. Try to trust.

"Hello, Inie? This is Kathy... I'm having a hard time."

My composure was fading fast and my speech was on the edge of disintegration.

Trust. Try to trust. Don't hang up.

Later, when I walked into the room where we talk, entered that space where I face all this, it was like receiving a physical blow. Glass was crashing all over the place and I could hardly walk, my legs were so weak.

But I struggled. We struggled together. There had been no writing down of the images to soften the blow. There had been no verbal exploration to ease the way. I was desperate and needed Inie's help and support.

"What's happening?"

Telling her was pure, raw and visceral.

I tried to talk but went down the chute — deep into my kid. Sweat was pouring down my back and my stomach was twisted into knots.

I screamed. I screamed my brains out and they ended up splattered all over the room. I felt myself kicking and flailing as I hit the floor.

And then something magic happened. I can't explain it very well, but when I came back together and could get refocused I was holding the child in me. I could feel her. I could feel the child crying and I held her and tried to comfort her. I felt a physical bonding with her and I felt she was happy to be held.

Last night I felt I was holding her when I went to sleep and I was holding her when I woke up this morning. She has been inside me as I've written these words. When I've felt the pain again I've held her a little closer and caressed her gently and the pain passes. I tell her she's alright now. She's with me.

"I don't feel the pain so much now," I told Inie when I left her.

"It's because you held her. You held the child and took care of her."

My kid is very weak and tired right now. But, she is. More clearly than ever she exists for me and somehow we'll struggle on from here.

It was not very long after that that I realized — became aware — that when I woke up in the mornings she was contentedly sucking her thumb.

The next day I wrote this poem — the first of several which seemed to emerge whole from me.

TWICE A CHILD

The broken piece/little person
The split/kid
The child in my arms.
Out of the box and into my life —
You're so young, so little.
You were too small then —
So fragile now.
How do I care for you—
Learn you/let you grow
How do we absorb each other and heal the split?
There is so much to learn.
And even more to pass through and leave behind.
I do not know what it all means or leads to —
For now, perhaps, it's enough/today/to·just lie down
And rest
To take a nap and feel
Calm
One with another.
Together/in my arms/child/me.

1/2/82

Obviously this process was having an enormous effect on my life. The way I handled that was to keep it contained almost totally between Inie and me and sharing a little of it with a couple of close friends.

I was married with two adolescent children and I found I needed my home space as a refuge from both work and the therapy, so I didn't tell them what was happening or that I was seeing Inie.

I was also careful to not allow it to spill over into my work space.

I hurt. My vagina, my rectum, my ego and pride — they all hurt. I think my sense of dignity is dead. I just want to stay in bed and keep the electric blanket on.

Rob wants to know when I'm coming back to work, back to daily crisis and counselling substance abusers. I reassure him and make him laugh on the phone.

Robert — my chosen brother. I wish I could tell him what's happening to me, but I know I won't. I can't. Instead I hide out in a few days of sick leave.

"Robert," I'd say when I'd get back, "I'm in a bad way. I'm in the ditch out here on Memory Lane and ripped up pretty bad. A case of rape crept up on me, on my blind side. I'm bleeding, see. . . and I'm going down hard."

"Heeeey! Not our leader!"

And we'd both laugh at the way he'd say that, making me sound like I'm infallible.

"For real, man. I may be dead for all we know."

"Naw. I can see your pulse from here. It's green."

"Robert. You're on the wrong side of the partition to see my pulse. Besides, I'm shooting myself over here."

"I'm not knowing what you're talking about. . . ."

It would make us both laugh.

We have a client whose mother always says that. "I'm not knowing what all this means." No matter what we try to help her understand about her daughter's $175 a night habit, she "doesn't understand."

"What are you saying. . . . I'm not knowing what you're saying." Rob would say that as he'd come around to my desk. We'd laugh at how crazy the conversation sounds. It's the way we tell each other that the situation we're working in is making us crazy. But he would look at my eyes to see if there was anything serious in what I'd said. And maybe that would get me through.

I wish I didn't understand. I wish I could handle this the way Rob and I handle the painful stuff at work. We talk it over for real, but a lot is handled through the private joking that's the safety valve.

"Rob. I think I'm in love again."
"Again? Who with this time?"
"I don't know yet, but I will any day now."

"Kathy. I was wondering if you could cut me some slack for a couple of hours? I'm still really bummed out about ——'s suicide. I need to be alone."
"Sure. You O.K.?"
"Yeah. Just cover for me for a couple of hours." "You know it wasn't your fault. You can't keep someone from killing themselves."
"Rob? This is Kathy."
"Kathy? You mean Kathy In The Middle Of The Night? That Kathy?"
"Yeah. It's only 3:30, man."
"What's up?"
"—— cut her wrists."
"What? Are you kidding me? She doesn't want to die."
"She cut her veins lengthwise. She cut them up." Silence.
"Shit. Will she live?"
"I don't know."

I don't want to go back to work right now. There aren't enough jokes and laughs to get me through. Not now. But I miss Robert. I wish we could just laugh together and it would get me through this.

Getting back to work was hard. I felt too vulnerable. I walked in the building and people began asking me how I was. They all believed I'd been home with the flu. I know they just care and are expressing concern but it makes me uncomfortable to have much focus on me right now.

And then when I stepped into my office there was Willie. Out of the blue is my old friend whose face lights up when he sees me. Willie with his soft Arkansas speech and soft brown skin.

"Hey," he said and smiles.

I smiled, too, but I couldn't keep it up and tears seeped into my eyes.

"How you doin , girl?" he said still smiling. He was happy to see me.

I reached out to touch him as the emotion welled up and out.

"What's wrong?" he said when he realized what was happening.

"I've been raped," I said. I couldn't believe I said that.

"Oh, Kathy. . ." and put his arms around me. "Let's get out of here."

He held my hand all the way out of the building and into his car.

Willie is an old friend I've worked with a lot. We've been through some heavy experiences with groups like the police department and it has made us close and trusting. Willie loves me.. pure and simple. . . no strings or complications attached. We are equals.

We were a couple of blocks away when he said "When?" I couldn't answer. "O.K. Bad question." he said softly.

And that was it. No probing, no questions. no assumptions. We had breakfast and talked about all the things we enjoy talking about. We both laughed some.

On the way back in the car he said, "Are you getting some help?" And then he went on to talk about someone else and a totally different situation.

"She talks too much," he said. "She doesn't mean to, she just does. Anyway, for me there are only a very few people you can really talk to and share the really personal things."

It is amazing to me that you could try for years to get some people to understand who you are and what's happening to you and that there are others who can understand almost without being told. Willie and I talked deeply about what's happening with almost no words. I have no idea how he ended up there on that morning but I'm glad he did.

Talwin. Everybody needs a friend, right? I couldn't stand the pain any longer so I took some. The label said for "severe pain". Well, it was severe.

I thought it would block the pain of this past week, the memories of my childhood. It didn't work. It blocked the pain all right. It dulled the sensations. I could feel its effects creeping into my arms and legs, making them heavy and warm. But it didn't make the emotional pain go away. It didn't drop a chemical curtain between my consciousness and my memory or fears. In fact, it seemed to release a flood of images I did not want to see.

I saw myself in a concentration camp with a number on my left forearm. I was very thin and exhausted looking. I looked at the numbers tattooed there and felt panicked and sick. As I looked I saw the veins in my wrist being cut, opened up by some invisible razor, and the blood began to pour out.

For hours there were horrible images and terror moving through my mind. It felt like being crazy. I didn't go to sleep like I had hoped.

I think it just opened the channels into the center of my agony. No more. It is as close as I want to come to being crazy.

Obviously I was struggling. I would have given anything for it to all not be true. It was like being an onion and being peeled and taken apart layer by layer. I kept wanting it to all be a terrible mistake — for it to be all gone when I woke up some morning. But with each new memory, each new level of awareness, it got harder to deny that I'd been sexually abused. The word "incest" made my skin crawl.

And all the while, at each new level, I found I couldn't really deny it because the physical feelings were too real. My own body was filled with the physical residue of the memories.

But if I could have denied it I would have.

I am very tired. I need more sleep. This child of mine needs more rest. She needs to get through all this and be allowed to lead a little more normal existence... to be calmed and cared for. I think I have a real need to do that now.

I reached new levels of awareness that I'd repressed a great deal of my past experience and that there was truly this child part of me which was split off — separated — and needed to be nurtured and healed.

Today, with Inie, I felt I really held my kid. For the first time she leaned on me a little more as if she trusted me. And I liked it. I liked the way it felt. I liked the way it made me feel more whole and solid.

If I had to explain it right here in black and white I'm not sure I could. I can say how it feels, but I don't know how to say what it is. It's like something physical which is warm and gently pressed against my body from my chest down my abdominal cavity. It feels real in my arms and hands and it makes me experience emotions which come from very deep inside me. I feel as though there's a bond, an emotional bond, full of love and care, that reaches in and pulls things out of me. It connects. That's all I can say. It connects and fits. Whatever it is, if fits into what feels like a hole in my insides. It is very comforting and calming even though sometimes it makes me cry.

Inie encouraged me to stay with the feeling that there really was a child and she helped me to understand that there was no one better able to heal her than me.

When during our sessions I would come back from that other space —

---

back consciously to Inie and her little office — she'd tell me "Hold her. The kid needs for you to take care of her." She took my arms and placed them around my imaginary child. "Hold her. You can take care of her."

What is it? I suppose it's explainable in psychological terms and I could give a basic description of it myself. But that doesn't do the job for me. I really don't care what anyone thinks of it. It feels like me. It feels like a small child who hurts terribly. She's frightened and needs to be cared for, to be held, and when I can hold her I know how she feels. I don't wonder what she needs. I know. I don't wonder how she feels or what she should do. I know. I'm not real confident about it yet. I don't know exactly how to react or respond in the long run, but short term, how to take care of her when she's in my arms. . . .that I know and I like the way I feel when I do it. And I, the grown up me, don't want to get real complex about it. I don't care much about explaining it. It's more important to me that I can experience the need to hold her. . . that my arms want to be around her and that my body wants to rock her gently. I wish I really could hold myself at age four, experience her falling asleep in my arms and I could feel the tension leave her body and see her face relax. I'd like to just quietly hold that part of me until she woke up and let her see that she'd been safe and that I hadn't left her. I'd like to believe I could see more trust in her eyes and in the way she allows me to experience her body. . . the extent to which she can make herself vulnerable to being touched. I'd like to think she will reach the point where she can just allow herself to be with me and just come to trust that whatever that means she will be all right.

What is this or who is this? It's me. It's the part of me that, when I was very young, stopped doing all those things. All these years I have known it was hard for me to do those things . . . to allow someone to really know me and to make myself vulnerable . . . but I've not realized the extent or all the reasons.

I've just known I've lost something, a part of me, along the way, and I didn't know how to get it back. Parts of therapy are awful... more painful than I could have imagined. And it is certainly showing me that I probably chose to let that part of me go ... I made a passage to a safer and saner place... and the price was leaving myself ... that little girl... behind. I could not handle the pain of her life and she probably couldn't find her way out of it. The solution was to emphasize the parts of me that didn't hurt so much. I think I selected out only certain parts of me and my feelings... I created a new package....a new person so to speak, and I guess parts of me, the child, got left out and behind.

And it worked a lot of the time. But I think all the pain and memories are still alive and well... stored in my body, my muscles and lungs, vagina, rectum and brain. Not looking didn't make them go away... no matter how long I managed to keep from looking.

I still fight looking at all this. I do not like the feeling of falling backwards in time and into an emotional swamp, even for the kid's sake. It hurts. It makes my body hurt more than I would have ever thought. And it scares me. I realize now that I can't do it alone. I think I've spent so many years working at not looking and feeling all this that it is absolutely against my nature to willingly do it now. To an extent I have to have some pushing to get focused and to move into the space where all this repressed pain lies. And I have to choose over and over again to keep trying to understand and resolve it. I have to learn to listen to my body.

The therapy was being remarkably forceful in my life. I continued to work, had a somewhat less active social and family life, but the major focus of my life was this process of unfolding and becoming aware of my repressed experience.

I found I needed to rest and be alone more.

Inie says I will heal. That the places where I feel the pain now will heal and the pain will ease. I believe her because we've worked at this for a while now and there are places which feel a lot better. My chest is looser and my speech is less difficult and not such a struggle when I try to talk if I'm emotional. Sometimes my legs feel strangely relaxed and loose but I don't really know why. At any rate, I am aware that my body is feeling different. . . . less tight and more at ease and comfortable.

I know that for all the times I've struggled with this. . . tried to handle this problem. . . I've not been able to get all the way through. I've needed Inie's help and support. So, I will keep trying. I will stay with this process/therapy/struggle as long as I can. I will try to get through it and be healed. If I have to make conscious the pain stored in my body and look at the memories I locked out in order to get to the child, I will try. Maybe I'm beginning to understand a new answer to the question, "Do I want to live?" It has been frightening to me when I have found myself thinking about suicide. . . about giving up. It makes me feel a strong urge to stay connected with Inie and her help because I don't want to die. But, what I think I'm finally really beginning to understand at a very fundamental level is that the opposite of death may be. . . . may have to be for me. . . . more than just living. It has to be being healed. Maybe as long as I'm divided. . . as long as I have this hole in me. . . I'm not really alive the way I'm supposed to be. Perhaps I didn't understand or value this third possibility as much as I might have and maybe it's taken someone else to make me begin to see it clearly.

All I can say is I will try. I will keep trying. And I know I have to do it straight. I'm not proud of using the Talwin to try to avoid facing up to it. That is not the answer and it's not even very smart, especially for me. I guess the only way to go, the way that really works, is to do it. Feel it, pass through it and heal up afterwards. I don't like it. I sure as hell don't like it. But I know now that I have to do it.

"You can trust the process," Inie said. "It will heal."

Trust. Keep trying. Believe.

I really do want to be healed and free from this. And I like how

71

I feel when I can get to the child ... my little girl.

"I love you." I told her that today. "I love you." I don't really care about the details. It feels good and that's enough.

And so we struggled on — me, Inie, and the kid. The process became that I'd go to see her, fall over backward emotionally, come out of it, try to talk through what had happened, and then let it all simmer internally for a few days. Then invariably I'd need to write. I spent hours forcing the current experience/meaning on to paper. I'd then take the journal entries to Inie and usually she d read them at the beginning of the next session. Sitting there while she read, the kid would start to squirm emotionally and we'd start all over again. Sometimes I woke up on the floor with no idea how I got there.

It was a gruelling, difficult experience. While I had no conscious memories of what was happening with my body while the kid had her weekly explosion, I'd had a concussion a few years earlier and knew what my head felt like when it'd been banged around, and that was how it felt several times when I'd leave Inie's.

And standing naked in the bathroom one morning I saw bruise marks from Inie's fingers where she'd apparently held me down. Looking at myself in the mirror that morning was like having another layer of the onion peeled. There was no way around it. It really was happening to me.

But the good part was, there was a tender, growing relationship with my little girl me. Inie was right. The process was healing.

Little girl. . . . I wish I could hold you and talk to you. I feel now that I can express some things to you by holding you, by feeling what I feel and by my words, but I still wish I could hear your voice and your thoughts.

I know that perhaps what you experienced was so physical and brutal, and that you were so young, that you probably didn't have a lot of words to even process some of what it meant. And I know you felt alone and silenced.

Did anyone ever hold you then and say, "What's wrong? Tell me what's wrong, honey?" Did anyone ever look at your body and see, really see, what you were going through, and pull you into their arms and let you cry and talk? I wish I could ask you and you'd tell me, but I think I already know.

I wish we could talk about some of this. I wish I knew where Aunt Ruth came from, and how you found her, even in your mind? Who did you see or what did you experience that brought her to you? She was so foreign to the world you lived in. I understand the why of Aunt Ruth, but I don't know the how.

Perhaps right now you can only communicate with me physically. Maybe that's the only way ever. Maybe we just have to do it through our common body, no matter how uncomfortable I get. So much of what happened to you was physical and it got stored away in me. If we could talk about it you couldn't tell me any more clearly than my own body tells me. Could you tell me more than that it hurts, that you're scared and you don't like it? I don't suppose so.

But, god, I'd like to hold you. I wish I could touch your face and take away your tears. If I could have you physically in my life right now you would love how you felt warm and secure and safe with me. Nothing would be more important to me than helping you feel as though you'd been found and safe, and I'd see to it that you were healed. I don't think I'd care a bit if it took all my time and energy.

And it would heal me, too. You'd relax and be able to trust being touched again. I would keep you very close to me and you'd begin to grow emotionally again. Slowly, slowly, you'd be able to move on into the rest of your life. But you would always have me to come back to. I'd always be here for you .... always. I promise.

I know that you are me. You are me as a child. But I am me, too, and somehow we must come together in a way that is comfortable and healing for us both. If that's called healing the split, fine, I just want it to happen. As things stand now, you are too young and full of fear. So I still keep you mostly sheltered at home, in my bed, or at my desk while I write. I don't expose you where you feel too vulnerable and frightened.

And me, the grown me, isn't always sure of what to do. I am trying to find you, to get to you and feel you. When I'm with Inie, when she holds me, I can feel you strongly and am deeply touched by you. The emotions I feel are warm and fluid and they flow out of me and over you and it's very healing. It makes me feel fundamentally good inside to be close to you.

Please don't go away. Last week somehow I lost you for a while when I took the Talwin, and it scared me. Big grown up me got scared and hurt and I couldn't make the pain go away. It was awful. I ran right into a wall of self-destructive thoughts and images and I knew it was wrong. I have to stay here and build this relationship with you. I have to give you time to learn to trust me and I have to work at trusting Inie. She will help us build a bridge between us. Please try not to run away. I need you and I want you. Together we'll be all right. If we can stay together maybe we can both heal.

Stay with me.
And I will try
To hold us both
Until
We can be together

Between us we have
A lot of
What it takes
To become
One,
Whole,
Real,
Balanced,
Happy,
Person.

Stay with me
Child
And I will try
To hold us both
Close
Enough
To me and you
That we won't come apart.
Stay with me.

I love high school basketball.

Last year some friends gave me a sweatshirt that said that. I love the games and being unabashedly partisan. I yell. I applaud wildly. I really care who wins. It's a cheap high. And an hour later it's gone — over — and life goes on.

All winter long on Friday nights, I go. It helps me stay sane. . . . releases my frustrations and each week I begin to look forward to it by Thursday afternoon. There are a bunch of us who go and we have beer and pizza afterwards.

Friday night it was Ashton vs Union Hills. There was never more than five points difference. There was one overtime, but my Polar Bears pulled it out. Fantastic. It was a made-to-order Friday night.

So how come in the middle of it all I felt it again? Right in the stands I felt the pain and discomfort. Pain, real physical pain went through my vagina in waves.

It made it hard to watch the game.

If you could talk, what would you tell me? What would you say?

I wish Aunt Ruth were here to help me. She would know what to do — how to hear you.

"Bring her to me," Ruth would say. "Let me see her." I can see you in my mind. I know your face from the pictures. Your lips are slightly pushed together and your eyes are big and watchful. Cautious really. I think you're about three. It's the age at which I wish I could get you. That's who I'd like to have in my arms and take care of. . . before there is any more damage or fear for you to overcome.

"Hello," Ruth would say. "What's your name?" But I don't think you'd answer. You'd just look at her for a while and then glance away in discomfort or to gather your strength.

Ruth would be patient and careful not to frighten you. She would know not to touch you too soon or to push too much for a response. Her voice would reassure you.

If you were ever pushed too fast I know what you'd say. "Don't touch me. I will hit you. I will. You'll be sorry." Those words have been going through my mind for weeks now. I can hear your voice as you say them. They are a brave attempt at holding your own and your voice sounds very young. In the end I hear you cry, unable to keep your emotional resolve. I don't know what those words are connected to in the past, but I hear them often lately. You are a scrapper, but I know you're just a child.

But I don't know what you would say to Aunt Ruth if she could tame you, get you on her lap and gentle you into trusting. How would it be if it got to the point where you touched her back?

I think you'd make it look like the touching was accidental or as if you didn't know it was happening. Carefully and slowly the distance would be allowed to close. And any uncertainty would make you withdraw.

And that behavior would be the real communication with you. Your clearest words would be in how long your eyes and face are guarded and how long your body is held tense.

I would like to have you — the child I left behind — in a total sense. I want your body, your tears, your laughter, words and voice. But I know it is impossible to go back, in reality, to the 1940's and retrieve all that. So perhaps the best and most real connection — the direct length between us — is how much I can allow the memories stored in "our" body to come into my consciousness. Maybe the real question is how well can I let loose of my need for control and allow you — my child — to release your feelings and experiences through my body.

Is that what we must do? You remember and I feel it and remember it with you? Is that what will bring us together and heal us? If I can manage to pass all the pain and tensions through and out, will we have said it and felt it together and grown so close that we won't come apart again?

I know that when I work with Inie and even some other times I experience emotions and feelings which aren't totally mine. That is, they don't belong to the adult me,, at least not in the proportions that I feel them. The fear is often so strong it's astounding. Somehow it just pours out raw. You had few words and thought processes to modify the pain, didn't you? What you stored away was probably pure emotion.

I will try to face what you feel if that's what we need to do.

Just give me time. I get very tired, and I need to digest some of this more slowly.

I want to talk to Inie about what has happened. Is this what she means when she says "Process"? Is this the way you'll speak to me?

Your face is very young
And your eyes are big.
I like the picture where
You look so free and happy.

Little girl in me,
I don't know why it happened.
It was madness —
Crazy,
It never should have been.

And now
We
Have to find a way
To come/be together
That allows us
Both
To Feel
Well and able
To go/grow away from there.

Don't go away from me.
I need you.
I don't know where we're going
But we'll never be in that place again.

While there was real healing going on, it was still a struggle to go to the sessions. During those times, I began to not only fall over backwards and down the emotional chute, but I also found it harder and harder to verbalize what I was feeling. It was a relief when Inie told me what she felt was happening.

"I think a lot of what you're experiencing now is pre-verbal. You seem very young. Even if the kid were here now, she wouldn't have words to tell you. She'd have to show you if she could."

It was very hard to have to go through the process of allowing myself to re-experience being touched, fondled, entered and stimulated. It would come randomly during the week and always when I'd begin the drive to Inie's it would grow in intensity. It was a difficult process to allow. It wasn't as if I was re-experiencing a broken leg. The feelings were not only painful at times, they were often painfully intimate. My sexualness felt very public even there in that private little room.

I'd leave there sweaty and wet-feeling as if I'd been in a wrestling match.

Trust.
Believe.
It was not easy.
And all was not a warm glow of love for my kid. There was also the struggle of new material, feelings and memories, reaching my conscious mind.

4:00 A.M. Quiet. Only the clock ticks at this hour. Yet here I lie locked in this battle with a set of emotional dynamics called "the therapeutic relationship/process".

For weeks whenever I've been alone — whenever there's time and space for my mind to turn inward — I've ended up in this position — watching my depressing parade of mental images. It's a little like being obsessed with a box of old photos, drawings, poems, written conversations, etc., and going back and back to it — trying to arrange them in some way which communicates some meaning, if only to myself. I keep struggling with the task without being sure why.

What drives me to do it?

What causes me to expend such enormous emotional and physical energy on this task? Is there some inner force which is pushing me to rebalance my emotional functioning? Somehow the ''real'' focus of my life has shifted and a lot of other, important things have become, at least temporarily, secondary. I still do those things but they are not what my mind turns to when it's allowed its freedom. Always it's back to the box and the process of exploring its contents and meaning.

Even my body is experienced in relationship to this box/process. I find myself wondering why my legs are loose or my arms feel tight at any given moment in time and relate it to what's happening in therapy. My stomach is the early warning system for my emotional changes and its signals range from faint nagging to knotted demands for attention.

''What's happening in your stomach?'' Inie asked. ''Nothing,'' I lied.

It's stupid to lie. It only makes things worse. But the real question is how did I get on these tracks and what propels me down them? It's not like I haven't been aware all these years of my stomach and what it tells me. I'm having this intimate, constant relationship where such processes have become the center of everything. This is a little like having an affair with myself. And every week I'm going to someone who helps me to focus even more intently on this affair.

''What's happening?''

''I don't know.'' And I usually honestly don't know.

''Just let it happen. Don't fight it.''

Once at an amusement park, I rode a roller coaster. I'd always known I didn't want to — but there I was with a ticket to every ride in the park — and I knew if I was ever going to do it, that was the time.

First they take the cart way up high to give it momentum. For me if they had pulled us part way up that first steep incline and then backed us down, I would have had enough. But once you're over the initial highest ramp, you're on the course — on your way — and you just hang on and go through it. Going through the corkscrew section where you're momentarily upside down was sheer terror for me. Other people screamed with delight. I screamed in raw, undiluted, panicked fear. Afterwards I could hardly walk. I will never ride a roller coaster again. Never. Period.

"Let it happen. Don't fight it," she says.

"No." If I don't say "no" out loud, it's what I'm thinking inside. "No."

"Just let it happen."

And then suddenly I'll find myself on the downside of the first, long, high, incline — past the last point of resistance — hurtling along toward the corkscrews where I'll end up screaming.

I understand what's happening but I still get terrified and need comfort and support. I don't like facing all this new information but at least I know Inie won't send me down a track where it's not safe. She'll stay with me. But I don't understand what keeps me on this roller coaster.

"Let it happen," she says.

Is that really an echo of some inner voice in me?

"What's happening? What's going on?"

Do I go to her so she will help crystallize my search — my own struggle with the contents of the box?

Lying here I think about going back — seeing her tomorrow — and my stomach twists slightly. My arms hurt and my legs feel tight.

"What's happening?" Slowly I feel myself begin to start up the incline. I fight it. I still fight it. It will be her voice which says "Let it happen", not mine.

I would get off if I could.

Meanwhile, life went on. I was still feeling somewhat depressed.

I'm uneasy, anxious — a sort of low voltage discomfort. I'm not sure what it is. My body feels tight and my mind is restless and fragmented. I'm easily distracted and find it hard to concentrate. Work is difficult.

I feel as though my energy is low — drained off, and I can't get regenerated and refreshed.

My stomach area feels tight and tense. I don't like feeling this way.

"You gotta loosen up," Val teased me after she beat me the first game of racquetball. She won by one point and was gloating a little.

I raised my arms to the heavens.

"Loosen up she tells me. Loosen up! Next thing she'll tell me to be nice!"

"No. Just don't be nasty because you can t handle my serve." She loves to win.

She beat me the second game by one point on a serve I should have had.

"What's happening, Mrs.E.?" said Robert. "You're not looking your usual, happy self today."

Cris, the receptionist, was more direct.

"You O.K.? You look uptight about something."

I found myself mad at David for not shovelling the driveway.

I think at the bottom line I feel so locked into the struggle/process of therapy. It's as if I'm aware there are parts of me I'm not familiar with, but I don't want to or can't focus on them. So the unknown makes me uneasy, I guess.

I'm sure some of it is anger. I know anger is probably a problem because it's so out of focus for me. Intellectually I understand it's an important feeling to be aware of, but emotionally I'm lost. It's like knitting with snow — I can't get it focused or make it compute. I keep trying to think it through but I can't.

"It's safe here," Inie says.

In my head I know that, but now when I think of pounding the floor in her office, I tighten up and my breathing speeds up.

"It's O.K. Let it happen."

I guess at the bottom I don't want it to happen. I don't want to feel what's in me. I don't know the depths of it and maybe can't control it.

"Let her feel. Accept her with all her feelings.

"I don't like some of what she feels.

"She has a right to her feelings."

What a struggle.

I found a legal pad on my desk the other day. It said "I wish I'd never told you that or that I could feel as secure again as I did when I told you."

I wrote it after the day the kid told Inie about the probing.

"You're safe here," she says. "Let it happen."

I did not want to face the mounting anger in me. I was passing through the initial shock of the sexual abuse and was feeling tender and protective of my child. But the anger was pressing for release and I had to begin to face it.

Today we moved some things around the office and in the process my shirt pulled out of my pants. When we were done Louise said simply ''You have scars on your back.''

It was meant as a passing comment. She is, to a certain extent, an old time Indian and is direct and open about her observations and thoughts. She would not have been offended if I'd said nothing, but my own silence was uncomfortable to me. So, I told her about having two spinal surgeries.

And inside I felt as if lightning, out of the blue, had struck too close. I felt a charge pass through me and twist my stomach.

''And anyway, I'm fine now,'' I said.

That was it. No big deal, but I realized that for a moment, when she first said it, I felt ashamed. I felt exposed and vulnerable. I'm still embarrassed that I was at one time valued so little as a human being that I was injured like that. And that's the real weakness in my back. Other than that it's healed.

I feel a remarkably deep sense of calm. I think I feel fundamentally in balance — centered perhaps.

At the end with Inie today I felt as if I'd been in an extremely deep sleep. My arms, legs and head felt heavy and it was difficult to move them. I could not rouse myself easily to get out of that, but it wasn't threatening. I felt very comfortable in my body as if my emotions and body were finely tuned or connected.

My body has stayed relaxed and calm for these few hours and feels good. I wish I could feel like this for a long time.

Something in me feels rested or replenished. Maybe this is what healing feels like.

My sleep is suddenly long and deep. This weekend I slept once for nearly twelve hours and when I was awakened by the telephone I felt as if I'd been in some very deep and relaxed space. I need time to come out of it. My body feels heavy, as if I'd had some strong medication or had just come out of surgery. I can't easily come awake and float back towards the sleep if I don't work at it.

I suspect that there is something pretty fundamental going

on — changing perhaps — in the therapeutic sense. Maybe I am going through the process of becoming new myself....maybe I am being born.

Once when I was younger I had a gyro top — the kind that had a wheel inside it that would spin if you wound a string around it and pulled it. It would make the inner wheel spin and balance the top for a long time. I liked the way it felt when I held it, especially when I would hold it off balance and I could feel the centrifugal force of it trying to right itself.

That's sort of how I feel inside. Calm. As though a balancing system has been activated internally. It feels
like what happens outside me right now won't knock me over — that the system will keep me balanced.

Right now there's no one in me screaming or saying ''Don't touch me'', or yelling ''Leave me alone''. But I can feel the child — my little girl. She feels near and calm and more alive than ever to me. Feeling her so close makes me happy. ''We'' are very content with each other at the moment. I like it.

Friday night I called Inie. I wanted to tell her how good I felt, but she wasn't there. It was just an impulse thing. I figured since I'd called her when I was miserable, that maybe for a change I'd call her when I felt up. I left a message that I'd called.

The calm feeling stayed with me and then something began to happen in my stomach late Saturday afternoon. I want to write about it not because I want to say ''You didn't call me back'', but because I recognized something which I think is perhaps important. In this case the how of what's happened is what's important, not the what.

As time went on, I was aware that I was feeling tighter in my stomach and I tried to think through why the tension was growing there. Perhaps if I had not felt so relaxed I might not even have recognized the feeling. I knew, intellectually at least, that either the message didn't get to Inie or she was gone, or there was some other reason why she didn't call back. I know that.

I have clients, too, and I take that seriously and I know her well enough to know how she feels, too. And besides, I told myself, it wasn't even an important call. It was an impulse — a little fragment of the total process that I wanted to share. I think I wanted to say "I feel better and I think you have helped me feel that."

And now here I was recognizing I was getting a stomach ache over this and it didn't matter if I wanted to or if I understood, at least at one level, that it was crazy to feel this way. I felt embarrassed that I even thought about it much, yet the feeling in my stomach was real and it wasn't going away.

I decided to try to figure out what it was — why was I feeling that way — and something really interesting happened. I was lying on the bed and tried to really figure out what I was feeling. I knew it was tension and the tension felt connected to the phone call to Inie, but what was the emotion I felt? I thought about talking to her because I knew that I could allow it to get in the way of my relationship with her which I feel has been productive and which I don't want messed up. Especially I didn't want it to get messed up over something this silly.

So, I thought, what would happen if I talked to her about it right now?

I was astounded that within seconds "the kid" was furious and telling Inie "You don't love me!" My body tightened and emotionally I was back hitting the floor and telling Inie I was never going to talk to her again. I felt a wave of childish anger and hurt come over me.

I don't know how to explain it more clearly than that. But I was me — grown up me — with an understanding of why the call might not have been returned and that I could pick up the phone and call again if it was really important. And at the same time, I could feel the child who was hurt and, I think, scared and maybe feeling a little abandoned.

The important thing is that after it passed the pain and tension in my stomach was gone. I felt more relaxed. That is why I wrote this down, because I want to be able to explore with Inie if what I felt was really the child's anger. Was the physical tension really the child's emotions, no matter how much intellectual understanding the adult me had? If I learn to allow myself to stay in touch with the child's feelings, will that keep my body this relaxed?

I think for the first time I've managed on my own to deal with the kid and what she feels. Maybe I've made an important connection here.

Well, so much for calm.

I'm sucking my thumb. Recently I dozed off and woke with my thumb in my mouth and just passed it off as nothing. Then it happened again when I woke up yesterday morning. And last night I wanted to curl up and suck.

I can't do this. I feel like I'm slowly being reduced to a level of immaturity where emotions and physical impulses are less and less in control. I can't stand it. This morning when I woke up I wanted to suck my thumb, for god's sake! So I did and now the emotion is surging in me again and it's hard to concentrate. How the hell am I supposed to live like this?

I liked the calm relaxed feeling, but I won't want to be like this. I've known for a long time that I felt like there was a very young part of me but this is crazy. Ridiculous! I need to get back on the tracks and go on with my adult life. I can't be all strung out like this. When do I get out of this damn swamp? It's one thing to have the feeling that part of you is very young, but it's really quite another to find yourself sucking your thumb.

This new development was very distressing to me. I was worried that I'd fall asleep somewhere and someone would see me doing it.

Inie was mildly amused, I think.

"Well, you don't do it at the office," she offered, deadpan.

"Cute, Inie," I said.

She laughed.

"No. Seriously. Let her do it," said Inie. "Let her have her little pleasures. You can allow that."

Somehow I was being outvoted 2 to 1.

A few days later I asked my mother if I'd sucked my thumb when I was little.

"None of my children sucked their thumb," she said firmly, as if I'd asked if I'd been allowed to play with matches.

The kid part of me seemed oblivious to my adult discomfort, and the sucking increased.

Later Inie told me I'd done it during a session while lying on the floor. God.

I hated therapy.

I can't sleep.

I keep thinking about dying. Suicide really. Part of the time I get settled out, but I keep feeling like I'm going down hard — fast — I can't get a handle. I'm not sure there is one and in a way I just want some relief.

Maybe I could be with Aggie and I'd be O.K. I just want to find someplace where I can rest. I can't keep doing this.

Peg Martins called from the press. She was under the gun on an assignment.

"Didn't you tell me one time you were an abused child?"

She needed someone to talk about the experience of child abuse as an adult. I owe her one since she's helped me out before. She promised I'd be anonymous.

Right after that I met with my boss. "We've reached break point and I hate to do it but we've got to let Rob go. I'm going to talk to him tomorrow and give him two weeks notice."

While he's talking to me, Rob's face appears in the window of the door — a big smile and wave that he's leaving the building — touching base. His face is open and happy.

I feel like hell.

And I can't even think about the program we've built. It will be a year's work through the shredder and down the toilet. It's damn hard to feel dignity and worth when this is how your work ends up.

I called Inie and she said, "Hang in there. Trust the process, etc., etc. I know what you're going through isn't easy."

I wished she'd have asked me what was wrong. I could hardly talk to her. She felt far away and like she didn't want to talk.

"There are probably other things pushing to get out and even if you can't hold on to the relaxed feeling now, you've had a taste of what if can feel like and you're going to make it. Trust the process, O.K.?"

Screw the process. I'm against the wall and trying to keep from throwing up on my own clients. I had twenty minutes to try to pull it back together before the next appointment.

I spent four hours with Peg. That was enough. She's a good person and I respect her as a writer, but doing the interview felt a little like throwing up in public.

Shirley may as well be going to school in L.A. Three weekends have gone by with almost no contact. The last time we had to really talk was about two months ago when I went there for a weekend while she studied for finals. Most of our conversation now is about her struggle with law school and my struggle with therapy here. I called her tonight until 1:30 and there was no answer. Now it's 5:00 A.M.

Yesterday with Inie was difficult. I didn't want to go in the first place. I'm finding it harder and harder to give up that kind of energy every week.

It's a relentless process of rearranging my schedule, going there, up the stairs, into the same room, and sitting in the same chair until I go under emotionally.

"What's happening? How's your mother? What's happening in your stomach?"

It usually doesn't take much to get me wobbling internally. Once the emotional shakiness starts I feel like I'm falling over backwards and down some chute or slide and I end up on some emotional/physical level which I call the swamp. The agenda there

— known locally as "the process" — is to muck around looking under old moldy logs, stones, etc. and see what's there.

The other thing that seems to happen is that there in that room the kid is stronger and often has her say. I'm not at all sure how it happens but sometimes there, my voice, words, thoughts, body and action become a child's. I become much less clear or formed as a person and what happens then is often fuzzy. Sometimes what I'm saying is coming from someone/where else other than the "adult" me who walked in.

"If I had been your child could you have loved me?" I remember asking Inie that towards the end of the first session and being astounded that I asked. But also a part of me wanting to know the answer.

"Yes."

The adult me says internally, "She can't really know that. It's all conjecture. She can only say that she assumes she could have — it's really a fantasy question — because obviously it's not possible to know. . .it's an impossibility. . . .so she can only guess at best. And besides it's an irrelevant question."

But the kid part of me is much simpler. She wants to know — yes or no. And probably yes is the only acceptable answer. The kid doesn't really care about all the adult intellectualizing. And the answer causes a closure, something gets into place — "snap" — like a snapper closing my jacket.

The physical and emotional seem very tied together and both are often more direct, raw, uncontrolled — something — than I'm comfortable with or than I normally am. I've literally thrown myself into the security of Inie's arms — away from some unknown fear — and truly not known why. I start to wobble emotionally and later I realize I'm on the floor and I don't know how I got there. Time gets absolutely lost for me. I keep feeling like I've fallen asleep but when I wake up I'm physically exhausted. It feels like I've been wrestling or rough-housing the way kids do and my head hurts the way it did when I was little and I'd bang my head on the floor. I know that's what it is. A couple years ago I fell and hit my head on frozen ground and it hurt the same way. I asked Inie about it and she said I'd bumped my head a little. But I think that's what it is. I know it is, but I can't get focused on how it happens — it happens there — and why I can't remember it very well.

I remember more about yesterday. Inie held my head so I couldn't bang it and I remember yelling. It felt emotionally violent — directed more inward than out — and it was a relief to have Inie help control it.

I remember waking up and trying to pull myself back together. It's hard to get focused when I'm so drained. I have to struggle with the feelings of trying to come out of a deep sleep.

My mind gets like a TV camera which is being bounced around haphazardly while it's running — only it's all inside stuff — going from one thought to another, one image or feeling to another. Lying there like that makes me feel like a pile of pieces. It's knowing I'm momentarily apart and there's not a lot I can do about it for a while.

Inie asked what I felt in my body, and I tried to think about that but the camera in my head kept wandering around.

Then I became aware — as much in a physical as in a mental sense — that what I felt/wanted was to be lying in Inie's arms, being held next to her body. It felt warm, soft and comforting to think that. It was just a dim, secure place to be/feel in my mind.

But then I had an unmistakable sexual impulse surge through me and like some emotional magnet, it pulled together all the scattered pieces of me and the impulse itself was painfully captured within my body. Immediately I wanted to bang my head and when I tried to control that I started yelling. I wanted to move next to Inie for comfort because I was scared, but I didn't want to touch her or for her to touch me all at the same time.

"What's happening? What are you feeling in your body?"
It felt like electric shock.

"Did she get excited? What is she telling you? What did she feel in her little body?"

I was trying to crawl through the carpet.

"What did she feel in her little body? I think she's told you something."

God. So this is the next stop on the process map — early childhood sexuality. Frankly I'd rather go back and suck my thumb some more — as embarrassing as that is. I'd prefer a simple oral fix to this.

So what do I know about this? Not much. Freud says it lasts until about five — then it goes into deep freeze until you reach adolescence. Sort of like the maple trees thawing out in the spring I guess. Then there's the complex stuff — folks wanting their mother. Beyond that I don't know a lot.

Maybe that's not what it is anyway.

"What did she feel in her little body?" Inie has asked.

I'm not sure.

In my fantasy or whatever it was — in my head — I thought about Inie's breasts and being held by her, I don t think it was very sexual in a "sexy" sense. I didn't even imagine her breasts bare. I think it was more softness, warmth, comfort and security. Being next to her, held by her, sounds safe to the adult me because I trust Inie and who she is when I'm vulnerable. (I know that if I didn't trust her I'd never go to sleep when I'm with her.) And the child me would feel safe being held by her and I think would feel loved there, within that safety.

But, what I felt was also sexual — a sexual impulse or response and I'm not very comfortable with that. "Her little body" is also my body. We're in this together and feeling what I felt makes me think about my own sexuality.

I can understand how things may have gotten confused. Given that children are sexual and given my experiences, surely there are elements of my early childhood which probably need exploration.

Inie said I felt sexual with my mother and then she turned her back on me. If that's true what would be the effect of that? Has that effected how I feel and who I feel sexually about?

I remember screaming "I don't need you! I don't need anybody!" during all this.

Is this what I do with my need to be held and comforted — taken care of — to feel safe? And that was O.K. until I felt the sexualness.

But doesn't everyone feel that when they're young? If we're all sexually feeling as children and need a mother's comfort, don't those things get connected for everyone? Wouldn't motherhood and sex be as connected as motherhood and apple pie? They probably are in reality.

As I struggle with this I realize that the problem isn't just that I experienced sexual arousal with my mother or with Ben but that it didn't get processed by anything other than a very young mind.

I'm not saying what happened was right. I don't know that I'll ever believe that. It was probably very confusing, physically painful, and a part of what I split off. And where did those feelings go? The pain and physical discomfort are getting into focus through this process. The confusion is probably coming out now in my feelings with Inie when I wanted to touch her and feel comfort from that. But I was embarrassed and ashamed.

Why did I try to crawl through the carpet? What am I uptight about? Does the early sexual experience block my ability to feel loved — loved just for me — and not sexually? If I'm not afraid of Inie and where she's at, then I guess my discomfort must be connected to me and my own responses. Maybe the question is how did I go from feeling comfortable with a thought to uncomfortable? What caused such a rapid and painful shift?

If that's the issue — if dealing with the leftovers of my early sexual past is where it's at — then fine. I guess that's the part of the swamp we're in right now. Inie says this is an important connection, but I'm lost and don't think I know where it goes from here.

93

Reading the article. . . .seeing it in print. . . .wasn't too bad.

I hope it might help some people deal with their own experiences and get through some of the isolation surrounding child abuse experience. I know how hidden and painful it can be.

I don't think I could talk about this publicly. Just reading some of it got to me. The paragraph about enemas landed like a spear in my stomach and made me yell. So, I know it's all raw yet, but maybe it will help someone else.

I read it by myself and then put it away. No one else in the house saw it. I think I need that space. I don't want this thing in my face everywhere.

Shirley called to say she'd read it and loved me. She told Dan it was me the article was about.

"How about we go to dinner?"

Ellen called.

"I just want you to know I'm thinking about you. I think you're very courageous and that your talking about it will help a lot of people."

We talked about it, really, for the first time.

"It's humiliating for me that it happened and that I'm having to focus on it so much now."

"Well, knowing about it just makes me appreciate you more as a person, and I want you to know I'm with you."

"Ellen, I don't want it to become a big part of our friendship. I need some space where I don't have to think about it, and the times we've spent together just laughing and teasing have been important to me through this. I wanted to tell you I did that interview just to be honest, but I don't want this struggle to become a focus of our time together. I need to be able to just play or whatever the hell we decide to do."

"Don't worry about that," she said and launched into a speech about the upcoming payback for what I did to her on her fortieth birthday.

"You're gonna get yours and you won't even know it's coming."

I like Ellen. She's crazy.

Sue called.

"I just want to know how you're doing with having that in the paper."

We talked for quite a while.

"You're dealing with some pretty heavy stuff, you know, and it's going to take time."

"How long? I really struggle with that. I wish I knew how long it will take. I think it would be easier."

"I can see where it might take maybe another year or more. It's heavy stuff, Kathy."

Crap.

Maybe it will get easier though, she said. Maybe once all the pieces are out things will lighten up in time and energy. And there needs to be a time of getting stabilized.

I think I want to talk to Inie about this. I think it would be easier if I had a date when I'd know that if we weren't done we'd at least talk about it again. Maybe then I could be free of the struggle in me every week about going or not going.

Tina is back.

Tina with dark eyes and a Chilean accent. My old college buddy turned sister and aunt to my kids, who calls me "Evert" and with whom I've had enormous political arguments. She and her husband, Mark, arrived this week from a year of living and travelling in Central and South America. One week ago they were listening to the bombs go off in Guatemala.

It was a typical Tina re-entry with hugs all around, stories of political oppression, border crossings, gunfire and no peanut butter. They called my house and discovered we were at Chinatown for dinner and joined us. The whole affair turned into a party.

"So, tell me Evert, do you have any more sense now than when I left?"

"No."

Tina — my verbal sparring partner. We both laughed.

After a few minutes, when the other people at the table were all talking, she leaned close and said quietly, ''I saw the paper today.''

My stomach sank. Peg had done a decent job at covering my identity in the article and Tina had seen right through it.

''Very gutsy.''

''You recognized me? You could tell that was me?''

''Of course.''

My god!, I thought. How many other people did, too?

I totally lost it today. I felt relaxed going to Inie's but soon after getting to her office I felt the emotional struggle begin. My stomach hurt and I had a hard time focusing outside myself or hearing what she said. I couldn't talk. She began to read what I had written about last week and my emotional level rose even higher. Then as she spoke to me I tried to listen.

She said something like ''Last week when you were yelling it was almost as if you had an orgasm.''

About midway in that sentence I think I realized what she was going to say and I lost my emotional and physical control. Orgasm?! It was the first time that thought was in my mind — at least consciously. Then I thought about my mother and if I could have felt that with her and it was like having my mind instantly and completely blown. It felt like every part of my body began to move at once and my next conscious awareness was of being on the floor with Inie holding me down.

''She's alright! She's alright! She's a normal, healthy girl,'' I heard Inie saying.

I remember her holding my head so I couldn't bang it and waking up much later. My arms, legs and head felt like they were made of stone they were so heavy.

I do not understand what happens when I do that and it's frightening.

Inie says I'll process this during the week. Right now I simply draw a blank. My mind is so bent I can't'' get it around that idea.

My guess is that I am — or at least a part of me is — about two or three years old. Yesterday after the session with Inie and moving to a deeper level of awareness of my sexual past, I went home to bed. I tried to think about it — what it meant — but I couldn't, so instead I sucked my thumb. I curled up in a ball and sucked as if that in itself would comfort me through this.

I decided to not fight the sucking anymore. Why struggle against that, too. Inie has said ''There's no harm in it.''

What would happen if I just did it, I thought, until I was — or she was — satiated? So for several dreamy, floaty hours that's what I did. I turned on the electric blanket and allowed myself to simply drift. Sometimes I'd fall asleep but when I'd wake up my thumb would be in my mouth.

Like some grown adult/child I moved off into a momentary safe, secure, warm place where I could soak up unlimited oral gratification. I was a child. I just kept doing it. I did it asleep, awake, with my eyes open and closed, and I stroked the silky binding on the blanket. I wallowed in pure, physical, oral pleasure.

I don't know why.

Maybe because that was easier than thinking. Maybe it's a way to put my mind into reverse and travel backwards to a time and space where there was no thinking — just physical/emotional feeling — and things either felt good or bad. Maybe it's that simple. Perhaps that's what I've gotten to in working with Inie, and sucking my thumb was safe and more secure than facing the sexual feelings I felt with her yesterday.

I have tried to think about what happened last week. It's hard. I don't think I can get too far with it.

I've only thought of the sexual past through images — some vague and some clear — and through the physical feelings which I've experienced during the therapy. When I connected the word incest with myself last fall it was a focus more on the relationship aspects than on what actually happened. The word alone was enough to stir deep emotions in me without going into gory details.

I'm aware of the feelings of being entered by fingers, a penis, and the enema bag. I can feel it in my vagina and my rectum. It hurt — sometimes a lot. I'm aware of trying to hold cold water in and feeling terrified that I couldn't hold it long enough. I have the feeling that during the enemas it was like being searched for something wrong hidden in my body. I remember being threatened with a hot poker from the wood stove. She said be quiet or she'd put it in me. Since she was entering my rectum with her fingers as she said it, I believed her.

These thoughts are nearly impossible for me to write. It makes my chest tight and it's hard to breath. It took me an hour to write the above paragraph and I don't think I could read it aloud.

Maybe I'm an emotional coward, but I don't think I'm ready to deal with what happened after being entered until I can deal with the idea of being entered in the first place. Maybe I did respond to my mother sexually with an orgasm but, if I did, it is now out of my consciousness. There is no physical, mental or emotional picture of an orgasm in my adult head. Yet obviously it's a very high voltage area which needs exploration. The whole sexual subject seems connected to raw nerves in me.

I know I need to look at it no matter how painful. I believe that's how the pain and raw nerves will be healed. But it was an experience forced on me in the first place and I guess I want to examine it more gently this time.

In my head I know I must have been sexually feeling, and that sexual responsiveness was possible and even probable. But in my guts the idea of having been sexually used by my mother is difficult at best, and impossible most of the time. There's not only terrible conflict about it but some ragged, torn wounds in my self concept, too.

I guess I'm saying I'm really not ready to deal with that yet. Maybe I need to try to gather strength by talking about the enemas, probing, pain, etc. first. I don't know.

Inie said the idea of an orgasm while being abused seemed to hit me like a lightening bolt. That's true. It felt like being electrocuted.

I didn't like that last session with Inie. The kid took over in an absolute storm of emotion, more forceful and frightening than I've experienced it before. I not only felt the falling over backwards down the chute, I felt like I was pushed.

There was an exhausting period of struggle to understand what was happening. It felt like hours passed while I was sometimes asleep, talking or unable to talk — feeling pushed hard by something trying to get into my conscious.

Finally I was relaxed, lying on the floor, and I could allow the feelings. Massive surges of sexual feeling passed through. It was unmistakable sexual energy radiating out from my vagina with almost shocking strength and as it traveled through me it made my skin tingle and the hairs on my neck react. The feelings were so strong I could not ignore them, and for a moment I felt as if my sexuality was suspended publicly in mid air and I panicked. I was too vulnerable. Inie was sitting on the floor near me and I'm sure I could not have hidden my reaction from her.

She took hold of my hands as if holding me in place and said, "It's O.K. Don't be afraid. Let it happen."

But I was afraid.

"It's O.K. if you feel that. It's O.K. to feel it here with me or even about me. It's safe to feel that."

I believe I am safe with her. And I don't think my feelings were about her. I don't think they were directed at anyone. I think those strong, forceful, sexual urges simply were — they existed — and in all honesty that alone is unsettling.

Maybe when I put the kid away all those years ago, my sexuality went with her. I don't know. I know those are feelings I've kept at arms length. When I begin to feel them I push them away before they get too close/conscious and I might respond to them. To feel them now even with Inie is uncomfortable in a fundamental way.

The other night I said something to Inie which is verbal short-hand for some of my painful feelings. I said "Don't hurt me."

I know she won't hurt me and that's not what that really means. Those words really mean "I'm scared. I have some feelings and I know they're sexual and they scare me. While it might feel good to experience them, I'm afraid of how vulnerable they make me when I feel them near you. If I allow you to know I feel, I'm afraid I'll get hurt.''

Those are feelings and thoughts left over from my childhood even though now I'm an adult and have more control over what happens to my body. My fear isn't based as much on real experience with the person I'm with, but on the need to limit the potential for someone else to impact me physically/sexually. It's an enormous risk for me to allow someone to know I'm sexually aroused.

I kid around with the guys at the office but if someone really comes on to me — wants to make me aroused — it's uncomfortable. And a lot of the women I know talk and joke openly about sex and I laugh with them and even make those jokes myself. On my birthday there were incredible jokes about sex and my supposed wild sex life. I laughed a lot. But real, direct, personal, turn-up-the-voltage sexual contact can be unsettling for me. And I guess by ''me'' I really mean the kid.

The other night with Inie I think I felt scared because I opened up and I couldn't hide from her. I'm not so afraid anymore about how she'll react if she thinks it's directed towards her. I think it's more fear of having someone see me in that condition. I think the fear is really that through those feelings someone could learn how to reach my emotions. If someone learns the ''combination'' I may end up defenseless. It's too threatening. It's hard for me to imagine I could maintain myself in such an ''open'' condition day to day. It's been hard enough to trust Inie week to week.

I've not written much about my marriage because it's been too painful and in many ways too distant from me and my real feelings. It's been mostly irrelevant to this process. But I need to say that it is a relationship in which I think these fears were reinforced.

This fear comes from my childhood experiences and I doubt that even I know the full impact of them on me. I think my kid is very present in my sexuality.

After I was about six I was relatively safe in a physical sense and I could allow more of my need to be held. I still need physical contact which is not sexual in nature. I think to a large extent I missed that part as a baby and child and I don't really know how to get that taken care of now. It's painful. I have learned over the years that while the need to be held is real in me, the need for sex is even greater in a lot of other people. When I encounter that it makes me feel inadequate and immature. So I've learned to try to not need to be held.

And that's the sad, damned truth.

I'm tired of all this.
I'm tired of going every week
To allow myself to be
Faced
With all this crap.

I'm tired of giving up
All the energy it takes
To try
To understand
Everything that happened
A long time ago...
Everything that's leftover/
Influencing me now...
Who I am
And what I feel.

Who cares anyway?

I am tired
Of
Inflicting awareness
On myself.

I feel relieved at having talked to Inie about this new sexual material. I'm not uncomfortable that the child part of me might feel a sexual response while I'm with Inie, but I'm not so comfortable that those feelings are felt within my adult body. If the child is to deal with this then we have to deal with those feelings through my body. When I think about that issue between the adult me and Inie I'm not as comfortable. I'm more than a little embarrassed and get uncomfortable about how she might interpret things. Mostly I was concerned about offending her.

I have tried hard to allow what I'm feeling to show and to be open to Inie because I believe that's the way progress will be made. It is not easy to allow the child in me to express herself sexually, or to feel and remember openly. Anyway it is a real relief to have talked about it.

I want to talk with Inie about what I would do if something — god forbid — should happen to her. I think I'd feel more secure if I had some idea of what she felt I should do under those circumstances. I've said to her a number of times ''Don't go away.'' In my mind that has mostly meant ''Don't get sick of me or tired of this process and just give up.'' I don't want to be alone with all this at this point.

We were deep into this process of going back to get my kid and taking her through treatment. I was finding that it took most of my spare time and the week of my fortieth birthday was filled with friends, teasing and practical jokes. In fact, I left Inie's, met Ellen, Sue and some others for a lunch celebration, and they had rented a male stripper who came to the restaurant.

Ellen had been right when she told me I wouldn't expect her payback when it came. There's nothing like being at the center of a spectacle to make a day interesting. There was a lot of laughing.

Today with Inie the kid was upset. There had been little time to be quiet and think — to process — and it had taken its toll. She was pressed by all the activity of three parties and trying to make sense of it all. She was also, I think, afraid of being abandoned.

Not very long after I got to Inie's a voice in me began yelling "I don't want you to go away," the emotional wobbling started, and I woke up later slouched down in the rocking chair feeling as if I'd been in a deep sleep and my cheeks were wet with tears.

"Let her get it out," Inie said. "She needs to get reconnected — to be with you. She was afraid she might have to go back in the box when you didn't have much time for her this week."

It was true. All week I'd felt the need to be alone and quiet — to retreat to my bed and let her suck her thumb and figure everything out. But it felt like every minute had been full of people and new experience.

"She didn't know about all those people who loved the other part of you," Inie said.

So I needed to let her lie down and rest after she cried in the rocking chair. I needed to let her just be and feel her. I fell asleep again on the floor and woke up more relaxed and rested. It was as if the child had finally settled down.

After that we talked about how the kid had felt the last few weeks as the sexual memories had surfaced and about what it was like when I was small and my mother would get me in bed with her. The memory of that is painful. The more vivid it became — the more I experienced how all that made me feel — the more I became aware of my need to just be allowed, or to allow the child, to be close, warm, safe, little and young. . .without having to fear what touching another person means or could mean. I need to be held the way I should have been. I need to be able to relax with another person without having to think about sex. I need to be free to have physical contact without that fear.

"Please don't ever touch me the way my mother did!" I told Inie.

"No. That would be very wrong."

During these weeks I have learned to trust Inie in a more fundamental way than maybe I've ever trusted anyone. I told her I love her and thanked her for not only what she's helping me do but for who she is.

Slowly I'm having pieces taken out of me — old painful pieces — and yet somehow I feel more solid and together inside. Something seems to be working. It's a relief.

My mother is back in the hospital and unable to keep any food down. I think she is very depressed and angry.

My father is very thin and seems overwhelmed by the struggle to cope with both their illnesses.

When I saw them yesterday I thought about how perhaps they will both die soon. That's a painful thought for me. For whatever else happened, their home, that land, is a source of strength for me. The annual process of gathering wood for the winter, planting, harvesting, the wild flowers blooming, the smells of the fall and wood fires are all part of my basic rhythm. The creek's continued flow and the shape of the hills — even the actual texture of the soil — is permanence in my life. I can't imagine them gone and that land belonging to someone outside the family.

But now when I see my folks aging so rapidly, see them both ill, I can feel that part of my life changing and closing. And I know they must feel it themselves. I think my mother especially knows she's going to die.

Sunday at the hospital when I stood to leave, her hand reached out in the air toward me in an almost involuntary way. It was like an unconscious gesture — a statement of need — and she wanted me to sit on the bed with her. She tried to pull me towards her. I couldn't do it. I just couldn't be that close to her even though I knew she was old, in need and dying. I'm not proud of it. But I just couldn't do it.

This morning in bed I was aware of my legs being tight — pressed against each other as if in a defensive position — and it was uncomfortable. But when I tried to relax them and move them apart — even a little — I could feel my emotions rise. My chest tightened and my breathing became more rapid. I tried to think it through, to understand what was happening, but it was mostly a tangled ball of feelings.

I think I need to explore it with Inie.

While the work with Inie was being helpful there was another side to that relationship which made me struggle.

I used to wish I wasn't in therapy with Inie because I liked her and wished we could just be friends. I wished we could simply enjoy each other — woman to woman — as peers. But now it feels like this whole thing — this interminable focus on my problems/weaknesses — has lasted so long that the possibility of that is gone. Now I just wish it was over. It feels like there is no way a normal friendship could ever emerge from all this. It's too out of balance. And that's too bad. I think we could have enjoyed each other.

I am beginning to feel an end coming. Slowly but surely it feels like I'm getting rebalanced and resolved. Slowly I'm feeling like I can handle my emotions again.

I give the time with Inie credit for that. I think she has enabled me to get more in touch with much of my early experience and to understand my present reactions and body feelings.

There is still work to do. Many thoughts and feelings are still charged with emotion. If my mother were to suddenly die or if the terrible childhood dream would come again, I'm not sure my new strength would hold up under any and all pressures. But I also feel I wouldn't be overwhelmed either. So, I will hang in until I'm stronger. And I believe that time will come again. Actually I've felt strong a lot in my life. This past fall things fell apart and now I feel I'm getting reintegrated again. The pieces of me are coming back together — in a different order or proportion perhaps — but back together none-the-less. Somehow — and I don't know how yet — this child piece is being folded in with the adult me.

My vacation began Friday night. Ashton won the City League title in an exciting, fast paced game. We had beer and a big pizza to celebrate. Life offers a wide variety of simple pleasures.

Saturday morning my dad called, upset that the doctors had told him mother can eat — there is no physical reason why she can't — but that she simply won't do it. Friday when he went to see her and she didn't appear any better he said he had hoped she'd be well enough to go home from the hospital.

"Why? So I can cook dinner for you and do all the work?" she'd snarled.

The doctors are all upset because she won't eat. Dad called me. I called the doctors. It became a real merry-go-round. The psychiatrist saw her Saturday morning. He then ordered a full suicide precaution at the hospital which includes a demand that someone from the family be with the person twenty-four hours a day.

I spoke with Inie before I left for vacation. She said to refuse to allow my mother to have a hold on me. I struggle with that. Logic tells me to go live my life. I've told ma and everyone else that if she has had a few extra days added to her life she needs to make the best of them. I know that she can be getting senile, or have a brain tumor, or the cancer may be breaking out in some other place where they have not yet detected it. I know all those things. But in my guts I feel like she is manipulating the entire family. I do not believe she is about to kill herself. I may be wrong. I do think she might continue to refuse to eat and die from that, which is the same thing only slower.

I think the psychiatrist should see her again, (he's cancelled his appointments and gone away for the week), that the effect of the anti-depressant medication should be carefully monitored, and that she should be watched. But, I do not think the rest of the family needs to become exhausted by being at the hospital constantly. The point is not for others to take responsibility for keeping her alive, but for her to do that herself. If she cannot take that responsibility herself, then she needs to be where she can be professionally helped.

I guess I'm angry about how this is all being handled and it's probably good I'm not there. I called my sister yesterday and she began complaining immediately that I was gone. I told her to sit on it.

I think I have to take care of myself. Maybe that's selfish of me, but I feel like I'm just now getting to the point when I can feel like I'm coming out from under the long term effects of life in that family and I do not want to get sucked into that swamp again. When I spoke with Inie Sunday night it helped to have someone to talk to who knows a lot of the past in my family. I think if I don't break the ties, at least to an extent, I will never be able to become the person I might be. It's like having a stone tied to me. Right now I feel as if I'm beginning to have a picture of what I might be able to develop into, but the old issues with my family, the old emotional pieces, keep getting in the way — at least they do if I allow them to.

There are some of those family dynamics which still shoot holes in me and that cut deeply into my self control. I can't go on from here if I have holes in me and as long as the old pains can get to me I keep having holes. I'd like to go on to graduate school but I can't move very far on it because I lose my confidence. I'd like to write, but something is blocking me. I think I'm at a crossroads where it's critical that I choose me. I don't know what else to do.

I have reread the past couple of pages. The first few paragraphs were written last Friday afternoon — waiting to have a glass of wine with Geri. I felt competent, productive, up because of my vacation, and as if I were in warm, loving relationships with friends that I respect and admire. My intentions were to go on vacation, look at graduate opportunities, relax, see some friends, and rest.

Last Saturday life again felt swampy even though I did things to convince myself I was a good, valuable person. I had to put energy into staying calm and — to an extent — justified.

When I read the part about my mother, I felt angry. I do need to keep trying to build my own strength because I am too easily shaken by things outside myself — especially my family.

I feel the need to write at a deeper level — to allow some new thing to surface or to pull something together. I don't know what exactly. But something is pushing — struggling to form and be released. Something.

I think it has to do with the sexual part. I've tried to think about why I reacted so strongly to the word orgasm. I know that even on the surface level, thinking of it in connection with my mother, it is understandable that I find the idea distasteful and mind-boggling. But it's more than that. It's disturbing. It's degrading. I'd like to believe it never happened.

There's a piece of the last session with Inie which keeps coming into my consciousness. I don't remember the context of this thought, but somehow I keep thinking about saying "Sometimes it hurt and sometimes I just did it hoping she would love me."

Sometimes when she touched me — put her fingers in me — it hurt both emotionally and physically.

And sometimes I think I allowed/wanted her to touch me, hoping somehow she would then love me the way I needed — that she would hold me and I'd feel loved. And maybe that happened sometimes. But I think it was more about having to meet her needs. It was not about my needs as a child.

I suspect I need to struggle with it because it feels the way it has other times when something needed to be allowed to come out.

My father cried last Saturday night when I tried to explain to him that the source of mother's depression could be something way back in her past.

He cried. He said he thought everything went pretty well between them until she got pregnant with me, and then she was mad and wouldn't speak to him for three months.

He was an old man venting his own pain, but still it hurt to hear him say it.

"And I don't know if you like your name but she said she wouldn't name you. I did it myself."

Here I am — all these years later — and what does it all really matter in the end? They really just get you here accidentally or not, and the rest is mostly up to you. So why did it hurt?

Who cares? Maybe the real question is why struggle anymore? Why put energy into focusing on the past? Maybe there isn't anything deeper. Maybe I should just let go of it all. Let it be done. Over. What difference does it make anyway?

Sometimes I feel like I'm leaving this place. Sometimes I feel like I'm flawed and no matter how hard I try to leave, the difficulty of my past will forever have the power to simply expand and recapture me. Sometimes I feel like there is no escape.

2:00 A.M.

My mother is dead. Buried today. Yesterday really. I am struggling to understand how I feel about that.

These last few days have been awful. I have hated it. She had what may have been a heart attack last Thursday late afternoon, was moved into the intensive care unit, had emergency exploratory surgery on Friday afternoon and never really regained consciousness. By Saturday morning her blood pressure had dropped to 36 over 9 and they had put her on a respirator. By mid-morning all the family had arrived and understood how bad she really was. Dad looked like a ghost. I kept pushing to get everyone to talk about what was happening. The resident doctor who was taking care of her was at one time my paperboy and thank god we could talk to him. He was willing to stop the super-medicine approach and to not put her on any more machines. All the doctors were very clear that she would not and could not recover. Somehow she lived through the night Saturday and on Sunday morning the resident said he was willing to try to wean her from the respirator. She lived for forty minutes after that. I was in the room when they took her off it and we were all there when she died.

That night I stayed with my dad and slept in my old bed in my old room. I thought about the old dream but it didn't come. My sister became consumed with a need to organize and control the lunch after the funeral. We picked out a casket. Nearly all the weird relatives showed up: an aunt who can't hear and talks endlessly about operations and other deaths, a cousin with one tooth who wanted to hang on to us for hours and cry because ''she just can't take it.'' (Then go home, a voice in me was screaming!) All four of us kids agreed we wanted to have a collective arrangement of spring flowers — something bright and uplifting. My oldest sister and I went to the flower shop the next morning and the clerk looked disapproving and said ''Whatever you want. . . . but most families have roses for that kind of thing.''

''Well, whatever you think is best,'' my sister said.

I could have smacked her. Within two days the small town mentality was suffocating me. The whole idea of doing what you want. . . . truly want. . . . is totally foreign. Jello salads arrived in a flood. It could make you queasy to open the refrigerator after a while, it jiggled so much in there.

Next came the visiting hours at the funeral home. There were lots of the old neighbors from my childhood and that was nice. They just look older. There were some people I went to high school with who just stopped by. The first one who came is considered the town harlot and she gave me a big hug. My sister disapproved. There were more relatives. Some are great but others are strange. There's one I call Sara-Out-To-Lunch. She's harmless but operates on her own set of tracks. If she lived in the city, she'd be a truly colorful bag lady. But in the poor, rural northern country, she's just crazy. When I was little I never saw her outside a lilac bush except in the wintertime. Sara came with her brother Lester the molester.

It was all exhausting. I feel like I've been mauled.

My friends began to come up from town. Four came in and, after I greeted them, I turned to my oldest sister who was standing nearby and said "Have you met these people?" In a very cool tone she said, "Yes. I've met them."

Carrie Campbell, who was smiling at her, expecting to be introduced, kept smiling and said softly to me, "She's never met me. She's hostile to you, isn't she?"

"Uh huh," I smiled back. "She doesn't like you either."

"I can tell," said Carrie, smiling all the while.

"Who's she?" said another outrageous friend, loud enough for my sister to hear.

At the end of the visiting hours we went to a redneck bar where a fight broke out. They said they'd make an Old Fashioned for Carrie, "if the recipe was on the label."

Tina announced she was going to stay for the entire visiting period at night too. I think she felt compelled to protect me after she saw my hometown. "You don't fit here, Evert."

Basically I hated visiting times. In the first place the body in the casket didn't even look like my mother and it drove me nuts to hear people say things like "Doesn't she look good?" and to see my loony relatives go up there and stare at her for ten minutes at a time. My brother and I had really advocated a closed casket but had lost out. I hated it. Finally Geri and Sue arrived to rescue me. My parent's house was full of out of town relatives and I got to go home.

"Now, before you go, who's going to bake the beans?" my brother demanded.

There were two cousins, an aunt, and two sisters who could do it.

"It will work out," I said.

I had bought the damn things on one of two major shopping expeditions the day before. All they had to do was open the cans, doctor them up a little, and put them in the oven. They were all staying at dad's with nothing to do until the funeral.

"But who's going to do it?"

I don't give a shit, a voice in me was screaming. "Get me out of here," I whispered to Geri.

"Did you get cream and sugar?"

"I got everything you put on the lists."

"Did you get styrofoam cups for the coffee?"

When I got into the back of Geri's car I began banging my head and yelling. Tina grabbed me and made me stop.

"Easy, Evert. Save it for after the fight over the plants and flowers." We all laughed to keep me from crying, it was all so stupid. We went for a drink.

The whole damn thing has been hard. When I came back to the house at one point from shopping my aunt had arrived from Hawaii and on the counter in the kitchen was a long white box about the same size and shape I've always seen in the nightmare. It made my stomach do a flip.

"What's in the box?"

"Oh, it's a surprise," everyone insisted.

It turned out to be flowers she'd brought. But that box made me uncomfortable.

Being in that building, the same one the dream always took place in, sitting with my family, looking at that casket. . . it was all hard. It was the dream come true except the struggle I've gone through in therapy the past few months has rescued me from the dream. I wasn't afraid of the dream becoming real. I just wanted it to be over and I could recognize that I felt relieved and that it was O.K. for me to feel that. It has been enormously helpful to have talked that through with Inie last week. Thank god.

I've learned something through all this. I think I've been enraged at my mother all these years for what happened. . . .even if I didn't entirely know it all consciously. And in the same way the physical stuff blocked the sexual stuff from my awareness, my anger at my mother has kept me from dealing with some other feelings I have, and to an extent, even recognizing them.

My oldest sister and brother are nearly as controlling as my mother. In the past week it was very clear that they refused to allow me any expression of what I felt. They would ignore or discount it, and they were uncomfortable with my friends who showed affection and focused on my feelings. It finally dawned on me that they did not want me or my feelings to get loose either. They wanted, insisted, that when I talked to them it was about cole slaw and paper plates. They wanted everything to look right, to keep all the secrets hidden, because to them, if things are hidden, everything is O.K.

As I got in touch with that I began to realize how much of the general family conversation involves controlling people. My cousin was going to the airport to pick up some people and there was a fifteen minute conversation trying to convince her about various routes to take and times to leave.

I began to understand that that is what I rebel against. I hate their efforts to control me. This may all sound very basic, but it's the first I've been able to see it. I've probably been too busy rebelling.

Now it's over. It's done.

I do not hurt because my mother is dead. At least the adult me doesn't. I hurt because through all this, no one in my family

113

asked me how I was doing or how I felt. They do not want to know.

The only exception to that statement was my cousin Paulie — my playmate who is a huge man with an eighth grade education and who is also seen as needing to be controlled. After the funeral, when the house was full of people and when I'd absolutely had enough, I went for a walk alone in the woods. When I came back after an hour, Paulie slipped out onto the porch and said, "What's going on with you?"

His asking made me have tears in my eyes for the first time during this whole thing.

He put his arms around me. "Don't hold it in," he said. "It's not worth it."

When I look back on the past few months when she was so sick, the past few days when the focus has been so intense, I know I have a lot to think through. In the end I played a major role in getting the machines turned off and making it possible for her to die. Was that right? Why did I do that? I think I know the answers to those questions, but I think I need to talk about it with Inie.

What will life be like now? I do not know what it would be like if I were not at some level engaged in a struggle with her to define myself. The impact of our interaction has been enormous. Who will I be if the struggle ceases and I become free to just be who ever I am? To a great extent I managed to do a lot of that, but she/they have always been around to judge and criticize. Inie has said to refuse to allow her to have a grip on me. That's especially true now. I got out of bed to write these pages because I was uncomfortable and needed to get this out. I should be able to just go to sleep like everybody else. But I feel young and vulnerable. Unsure. And I feel myself struggling to keep my emotions under control until I can get to Inie where the kid will be safe.

I'm deeply grateful that I am as resolved about all this as I am. I think I/we found the exit from that past just before the roof caved in.

I'm extremely tired. The emotional process of my mother's death, the funeral, and my efforts to support my dad have left me drained. I don't feel much, distant from even myself and just wanting to rest and be quiet. Last night I went to bed at 9:30, curled up around Aggie's sweater and sucked my thumb. It was a retreat.

I dreamed a lot but I don't remember much of it. But it was like last fall when there was so much stress and there would be a night-long jumble of images and situations rumbling through my mind. Off and on I wake up, suck my thumb, and cling to the sweater.

It is hard to relate to people. Too many people want to talk to me about deaths they've experienced, hug me, and take care of me. They assume too much about me and my mother. I just want to be left alone. I need to think — write in the journal.

Work is no relief. After two weeks off there are too many clients, phone calls, paper work and funding problems.

My head hurts.

I'm hanging on emotionally until I can get the kid to Inie — where the feelings inside me will become known. Last week I didn't feel much at all until I was on my way to Inie's and then they became uncontrollable. I arrived there holding my stomach and the kid cried for a long time.

There had been no room at all for my kid during the week with my family. There was instead a great effort to keep a lid on all emotions. My family demanded, through their behavior, that I be anything but a feeling kid. I think the kid cried for that, too. And for the relief of finally getting to a place where someone would allow her to exist. She cried out of the same relief you'd feel if you'd been held under water until it felt like your lungs might explode.

I wish I could enter a period of no more new emotional experiences, lots of rest, and a chance to get stabilized. My child needs to feel secure enough to just rest and play.

I've tried to talk with Inie about the end of therapy. I guess I think I'm supposed to. Someone told me she is very busy and under a lot of pressure from too many clients and too little free time. And now I feel guilty and like I should be handling these things myself. But part of me knows I'm also not ready to stop seeing her. It's painful for me to think about not going and I know that last week the kid would have been wild if she couldn't have seen Inie. I'm scared. I know the goal of therapy is not to stay in therapy, but to move on, but I also know I'm not ready to do that yet, but I don't know what to do with the guilt either.

Nothing is simple anymore.

It is probably not too surprising that when I tried to talk to Inie about this she told me she would make the decisions about if she was too busy and make whatever adjustments were needed and that I needn't worry. I also remember sobbing on her floor that "MMMy mmother died and I'm scared and I don't want to go out there all by myself."

God loves Inie. She simply allowed the kid to have her say, to cry, and rubbed her back.

"You don't have to. You're not alone any more," she said quietly.

In a way it's a relief that my mother is dead, but still she was the kid's mama.

It's true. Nothing is simple anymore.

I had an appointment in the south end yesterday in the late afternoon and couldn't find the address. I finally got so frustrated I gave up and called Geri who lives near there but she wasn't home. Then I drove past Inie's and then went to Tina's and when I got there I began to cry. I don't know why. Tina was fine about that, but I don't know why I cried. Later that night I woke suddenly with my heart pounding. As I lay there I began to hear what I have come to know as the kid's voice screaming, "I didn't kill her!!"

Looking back now I can see that if the adult me could cop out by worrying, if an adult, grown professional was too busy to see me, the kid could not. She focused on guilt and fear of loss in their pure basic forms. I dealt with them sideways through my concern about taking up Inie's time and resisted facing the kid's raw emotions.

This isn't comfortable in this place
It's not easy to be
Here
Waiting for direction to occur—
For my person to form.
I am. I'm here now—
Working, struggling, searching for clarity,
Yet I know that I am not
The person I will become.

I can sense me changing—
Having fallen apart
And allowed someone else
The extreme permission to sort through my parts—
I am changing.
And I will not be the same
Person/child/daughter/I was
When this began.

And it's not easy
To be waiting here,
Being patient
Holding my ground
Against all the forces
Inside and out which
Demand/urge/push/shove/expect and tempt
Me to be
Always adult/formed/together.

There is a mean wind which often blows
Through me and across my spirit
Which says
    You should be more together.
    And even if you're not perfectly balanced You should
    present yourself
    Act as if you are.

It is not easy standing here
Waiting for my child to grow up.

I think this period for me is like having decided to take a long journey by canoe — and right now — today — it feels like the first few minutes on the water. It has begun. This journey is not well defined — perhaps it's more like the decision to travel around for a while — but it is beginning.

This last six months has been incredibly eventful and all that time I've been working through the past — physically feeling things from the past — learning to understand myself a whole lot better — and living intimately with an imaginary four year old.

Then came March and death and now I think I understand it's over. The target of most of my life's frustration has died. And for quite a while I've realized that that anger against the past has been partly how I formed myself — my rage against the past was at the center of my definition. And now — mostly through the therapy — it's gone. Things have been rearranged.

Now here I am in the canoe — not knowing where I'm going. Life could be worse than a canoe and a four year old.

Except two days ago the kid threw a fit and refused to get into the canoe and nearly put us both into the water. She refused to leave therapy. So in reality we are really just mucking about in the backwaters. But for now that's good enough. It's a beginning.

I guess I may as well write about this. I'm sick of the kid. I'm tired of her demanding that she be so much at the center of my life. There isn't a day that goes by anymore but that she's scared, frustrated, angry, tired — something. She can't just sit in the canoe. Consequently, we're going nowhere because we spend a lot of time and energy keeping the canoe from tipping over.

Now she's into sex. Last time with Inie I couldn't get focused. It was like the emotional counterpart to when you don't feel good — a general feeling of being out of balance. The kid was out of sorts. She was tired. She felt cold. She wanted to lie down. I sat there feeling all those things. I could understand it's the child in me. I could understand she'd had a hard week, too, and now she'd like to have her say with Inie.

"Just let it happen," Inie says.

Right. Just let her do her own thing. Let whatever I'm feeling come out. Got it.

But then the kid starts wanting to lie down with Inie. She wants to be held, comforted, warm — all those good things.

However, there's beginning to be a small war. While there may be a split here — there's both me and the kid — there's only one body and it's mine. It belongs to me — big me — and I have something to say about who it lies down with. The kid has no moderation. She just wants, and I can get fairly uptight with her.

There is no conscious dialogue while all this is going on — it's feeling — but if we did talk it would go something like this.

"Look kid, we're not going to lie down with Inie. See, I'm holding you and you're going to feel warm and safe with me. Just relax."

"No. I want to lie down with Inie."

"Just hold her. Let her relax," Says Inie.

"See kid," I tell her. "Even Inie thinks you should stay here with me and relax. Just settle down and we'll be fine."

"No."

I feel a flood of images of what it feels like to relax and lie calmly with another human being. The kid feels the desire for the warmth of that.

Suddenly my body tightens up, my head starts moving from side to side, and I'm kicking my feet. I can't stop it and then — pow — it's orgasm time.

I can't believe it. For someone who dislikes going to therapy, I like having orgasms there even less.

When I got myself back together, Inie said, ''What did she tell you?''

It was hard for me to talk about it — to say it.

''Can you tell me what the kid told you?''

''I keep getting mental images of lying next to you, and then I felt sexual feelings.''

Inie is cool.

''You know,'' she said, ''small children are sexual, too. They masturbate a lot, for example. At least she's a good healthy kid.'' She chuckles and smiles when she says it and it eases things a lot.

It's hard for me to talk about all this. And this kid is giving me fits, but perhaps if I listen she'll teach me something about my own sexuality.

She's saying she can have sexual feelings if she wants to. And that she'll be sexual if she wants to — that it's natural for her.

I do not recall having an orgasm during the abuse. There's just not a connection with that thought. Mostly I remember the feelings of being entered.

But what I felt the other day was an orgasm — inside, vaginal, small/light, but definitely orgasmic. It was maybe what I felt when I was young.

''Kids do it in places like shopping carts when their parents take them to the store and they embarrass everyone but themselves,'' Inie said with a laugh. ''They're just not uptight about it.''

And I think the kid is helping me understand something else too. Maybe I've blocked a lot of the natural flow of my sexual feelings in order to block out the pain associated with it. But that must block out the pleasure, too.

The kid does it for pleasure. The kid understands pleasure.

I guess I need to listen to her no matter how uncomfortable lt makes me.

But still I get tired of a wet canoe sometimes.

Clearly I had my ups and downs — sometimes day by day — sometimes hour by hour. But the constant element was the commitment to staying with the treatment process and getting resolved. That never wavered. I hated therapy but I never thought about running away from it. I wanted this whole thing over and done with as soon as possible and I worked hard at it. My attitude was "let's just do it no matter how much I complain." I probably asked Inie if we were done each of the first twenty-five sessions.

I don't know if I can live with you.
You are too strong,
Demanding/free/little and vulnerable.
And you stick to my consciousness like glue.

Months ago on a painful night
You were there.
Sue said "Do you always hold yourself like that?"
My arms were folded unaware across my chest —
While I talked of my childhood —
As if to comfort myself.
But I did not know you then.

"Let her out. Hold her," Inie urged.
I didn't understand —
Couldn't feel you at first.
Now you seem to come at will.
Your will.

You suck your thumb.
Some days at work — when you get tired —
You just want to go home —

Home where a door can be closed.
When I/we get into the car
You get impatient and want to hurry up
So you can get there and snuggle in
And rest.
"Let her do it," Inie says.

You bang your head,
Throw tantrums,
And now you're into sex"
The other day you turned my body, my vagina, into a
little fish
With my insides like its lips —
Coming to the surface of my consciousness and gulping
for air
Until I could feel.
And then you swam away to god knows what else,
Leaving me to explain the ripples on my surface.

I don't know if I can live with you.
You're very complex.

There were new clouds gathering on the horizon; the relationship between client and therapist came to the foreground and demanded attention.

I do not think Inie wants to see me anymore. I feel like I'm supposed to stop going to see her and that it's taken me awhile to figure it out. It feels like she's tired of all this with me. There is probably no graceful way out for her. Maybe the client is supposed to have the brains to know when it's done and simply leave.

I feel like a jerk. An asshole. My feelings are hurt — not so much because she's probably ready to hang this up — but because I'm so damn dumb. I'm embarrassed.

I think I wanted her to love me and that's what's really embarrassing. She can't be loving everyone who goes to see her. That's not what it's about. Her job is to help you get your stuff out on the table and look at it and she's done her job. It is now my job to leave in a way that allows us both some dignity.

I'm a little short on dignity right now. It's been hard to sustain a relationship in which I've never felt like an equal. I understand that that's the nature of the beast when it comes to therapy, but it's still hard on my ego. It's very hard to leave my own clients and go suck my thumb in front of someone whom I could normally approach as an equal. There's not much dignity in being dominated weekly/daily by a four year old. I'm sick of it and frightened by the kid's need to go every week and be touched and held. It's time to grow up and get some of those juvenile needs under control.

I don't feel too hot about myself right now.

Love doesn't do it. Love, concern, patience, support — all those things don't do it. What makes a difference is if you — the individual — decide you're going to get it together. And that's what I had figured out in the beginning — when I was young. I waited around wanting my mother to love me for years and the sad truth is she never did. And that's my problem. My head tells me to hang it up and go on but I've continued to hang on to an infantile concept of love. I've had this idea that if someone would finally love me the way I wanted to be loved when I was a child — that then somehow everything was going to be O.K. Whatever that means. I would be happy. Probably ''happy'' isn't that pie in the sky I wanted anyway. It's probably just the absence of feeling like an asshole.

It's time to tell the kid to straighten up and for me to start paddling my own canoe. And I can understand how Inie's probably sick of all this, too. I feel stupid. I often feel this way with middle class folks also. I end up feeling like a social jerk because the signals — the messages about what's socially acceptable — are too subtle for my working class perception. I don't get it that a certain subject or action is taboo because I don't understand the signals. Oh well, I was never in therapy before either.

Actually — in all honesty — what I really wanted was to be able to believe Inie not only loved me but needed me. She doesn't "need" me. In the first place she has her own family and friends, and in the second place she has all the other clients she probably wants. She does not need a relationship to me. If she needs anything from this it's probably a sense of conclusion. She may well need her work and therefore need clients, but she surely can't need the amount of money I pay her.

I guess I really feel no sense of control at all in this relationship.

I am frightened of this relationship, Inie and the kid. They are both stronger than I am. I do not like it that I need either of them even though I do. It is too threatening to stay here. I feel very ambivalent and uncomfortable. I feel very little dignity and self-worth. I feel stupid and inept. I know the therapy has helped me in a lot of ways, but it's too painful now. I feel like nobody.

I feel tremendously relieved after having worked things through with Inie. We talked about how I felt about her being busy and about my feeling that I should probably stop going to therapy. I think to the adult me, that all seemed logical but the kid was going crazy. I think I was trying to be somewhere that I'm really not yet. I feel physically different knowing I don't have to face things alone.

If I could be assured that life would be a lot calmer I could stop seeing her, I think. Certainly I could cut way back. But I think I'm like a dog that's gun shy. If someone had told me six months ago that I would go through everything I have experienced during these past few months, I don't think I could have believed it. I know I am not ready to go it alone. Not yet. I need the safety and security of knowing there is some emotionally protected space where I can rest and try to understand it all. Through a lot of intense sessions most of the painful pieces have been placed on the table. Those pieces may or may not be taken care of and I think I need time to feel that I can deal with them and stay balanced.

"The child is still needy," Inie said.

It's true. She needs to be allowed to experience being secure.

In a way I wish that wasn't so. I wish I didn't feel so divided and that the adult me was free to just go on and live my life. I wish I were a whole, grown person who didn't have to feel what I feel. Intellectually I think I understand what's happening — all the stuff about people becoming split and needing to reintegrate. Emotionally I feel shaken. I wish sometimes I couldn't feel the kid part who wants to express herself — who sucks her thumb and cries. The last few weeks I have strongly felt the need to go back to see Inie and when I get there the kid's emotions take over and she has her say. Sometimes it's frightening. Sometimes it's a relief. But it seems it has become necessary.

The thing I sometimes struggle with is how can all this be so real? How can there be two such strong parts of me? At times it almost feels like someone else is in my body — someone else with thoughts and physical feelings. And that someone else is definitely younger. . . . more frightened and in need of the security of the time with Inie. The adult me could probably make it. The kid needs warmth, security, protection, and freedom to be. And I guess I have to just allow that. I don't know what else to do.

7:00 A.M. Thursday: Describe how you felt during the last twenty-four hours. (It was better than throwing my head through the picture window or chewing a leg off the dog.)

I awoke depressed. It was Robert's last day at work. I really don't want to talk about it.

By the time I got to work there was a message that he wouldn't be in. He would call later. Paul came into my office immediately and scared.

"Rob took off last night with his bonus check and my car. He never came home."

Robert. Out of work and afraid of what the lack of a job would do to him. Robert. . . three years off heroin and becoming an excellent counselor. But he's uptight inside about what it will be like back on the streets. Robert — my chosen brother.

It was as if a chain saw — the one which tore me open when

Aggie died — took a swipe at me again and narrowly missed my stomach.

"He'll be O.K." I assured Paul. "He's already called in."

Every telephone call all day tightened me up.

"I just hope he didn't go back to Taylor Heights," said his older brother, Don. "That's where he went down before."

Rob won't do that, I told myself. He's got too much going for him. He's a beautiful human being. He's stronger now. But still my guts hurt.

Clients came out of the woodwork all day. I went to court, held someone while they cried, and worked through lunch.

I heard from Rob.

He's a mess. Mr. Space Cadet. He's out in the ozone on speed. Fuck. So much for our team and all that good stuff. It felt good while we were saying it. But there are tracks — needle marks up his arm and into his brain.

I was very down when I got home. . . .

I called my father. He was even lower.

I called Shirley. She didn't answer.

I called Tina and couldn't talk.

"I'll come get you," she said.

We drank beer at the Vintage Bar until they finally closed the place. We talked about my job, why I seem to have no capacity to operate on less than eyeball-to-eyeball range with life, and about sex.

We decided it's probably a nearly impossible job and I'm probably too stupid to quit. We figured I operate the way I do because I have little or no basic belief that I am loved or lovable just for who I am. And that I'm very naive about sex — mine in particular — and that perhaps my best hope is that the kid in me will continue to grow — that I will pass through a second adolescence — and maybe I'll get another chance to figure it out.

"Or you could just screw a lot of different people or read a sex manual," Tina concluded.

We were mildly drunk. It felt good.

Robert is my chosen brother.

Robert.

His voice sounded shaken on the telephone.

"It's really hard, you know. It feels like one hit after another. Now it's hard to get out of the hole."

"You can do it, man."

"People. . . .the people I'm living with don't understand what's going on with me."

"I love you, Rob."

There was a tense silence on the other end. We have been so close, so open and now there has been this chemical filled space.

"You're the only one telling me that. . . ." It was painful to hear his voice crack with emotion.

"Maybe you need to look at if you're willing to allow anyone to say it to you. Remember we've talked about how you have to struggle to allow that — to trust people? You have to risk, man. It's too hard alone."

I was hoping he would inch a bit closer. Trust. I know Rob. He was checking. And he's terribly embarrassed by his condition.

"I'll call tomorrow," he said when he finished.

He was touching base. He needs to know someone believes in him.

"You need to take care of yourself — see to it that you're getting what you need emotionally," I'd told him.

"I'm really hurting," he'd said.

He has what it takes to put himself back together and my guts tell me that what I need to do is stay with him. One of our board members saw him enter and leave a dope house and came to tell me.

"I know. And all I can say is I believe that while Rob was working here he was clean. I think you either hire people who don't abuse and take what knowledge they bring, or you hire people who have abused and understand who they are. I can tell you Rob's experience has been invaluable with clients. When I slip up, I don't have his particular problem so my problems may take different forms, but I do slip up. At this point I'm going to take the attitude that he's had a slip, but I'm not ready to say he's lost his usefulness.''

Painful as it is, my bet is still on Robert. If he doesn't make it, it won't be because he felt that I too didn't value him or believe in him anymore. It would be neat and clean to walk away and look like a fucking saint.

''Looks like the right person stayed on the job,'' the board member had begun.

God, people can be simple.

Life was not exactly a clear, bubbling brook for me at that point. It felt like a lot of the people I cared about were struggling, too.

But true to form, the process — the relentless course of therapy — marched on, no matter what else was happening in my life.

I want to write about my body — partly to explore what's going on — but mostly so it's written down.

As the therapy has progressed, I've felt enormous tension leave my body. I think some of it has been stored in me for years. Sometimes my legs feel surprisingly relaxed to me.

I still feel tension in my forearms, mouth, lower legs, and neck. I don't feel it all the time but I'm aware that's where it's still in my body.

I have felt enormous relief in my stomach, hips, legs, vagina, rectum, and back. My chest is remarkably less tense since I've struggled through the memory of having the knife on my chest.

I have always slept with my legs drawn up and pressed together. Several weeks ago I realized I felt discomfort when I would move my legs apart while lying on my back. This isn't always true but sometimes I can feel the emotion rise in me as if by doing that I am somehow emotionally/physically exposed to some danger.

I talked about it briefly with Inie and it diminished. And I recognized that I always keep my legs touching in some manner. Even when they are open I keep one folded up so it touches the other.

I've tried to think this through. I don't like the tension in my life. I've gone for long walks trying to release it. When I think about what it must have been like for the kid to lie down, I get emotional and I simply stop thinking of it. It's a little like having my mind change channels. But the tension in my legs remains.

It is beginning to be close to the time for David to leave for the Air Force. He has stayed with my father a lot during the past several weeks and last night when we left my dad, he got teary eyed. He will miss Dave. Dave has been very good for him. But seeing my dad react that way got me in touch with my own feelings. I will miss Dave too. He is a soft spot in my life and we go to the movies and sometimes the basketball games.

I do not like this long string of losses/people leaving my life.

Almost every night I'm aware that the kid and I ride home from work together.

It's when I can tell what's going on with her. I can feel if she's upset, tired, playful — whatever. Sometimes she just rides quietly and looks out the window. But I usually feel in touch with her then.

When I was with Inie the kid again had her say. This time it was the tension in my legs which became the focus. It was painful as they tightened up and I realized I could not keep the adult part of me in focus. It was like one of those black and white, foreground/background pictures which either looks like two profiles or a flower vase — but you can't see both at one time. I couldn't keep the adult me in focus.

Later my skin and muscles between my abdomen and knees became very uncomfortable as if it were over-stimulated. That feeling grew and grew and then I could feel hands on me, hands rubbing me, and then as if stimulating me with only fingertips — very lightly.

I couldn't put my legs out straight without causing the tension in me to explode in intensity. It was very unnerving and threatening. Inie encouraged me to "stay with it."

The area of my groin became hyper-sensitive and now I think having my legs drawn up was a way to protect that part of my body. It became too much both emotionally and physically to expose it by putting my legs out straight.

Then I felt the hands touch my legs and groin and there was pain in my vagina. That's all I remember. Afterwards my legs felt tired the way they would after the first long bike ride in the spring. My skin felt like it had a case of the jitters and needed to calm down.

The next morning those feelings were still there and I stayed in bed for a while. I just lay there quietly and got in touch with the feeling of my hands just lying on my skin. I think my skin needed to be calmed. I could again feel how sensitive my groin area is, even to my own touch.

Riding home from work a few weeks ago I had a startlingly clear picture of my kid pop into my head. I was driving on the expressway, up a long hill past the downtown area and I could see the kid for a moment perched on the edge of the passenger seat. She was turned slightly away from me looking intently out the window at the city. She was about four or five and had on a grey wool coat. Now when I pass that spot I can see her and often feel her mood.

About a week ago I decided to say something to her. I was feeling relaxed and playful and said, "Well, kid, what do you want to do?" The weather was breaking for spring and I was thinking I'd like some ice cream.

But in my mind the kid never turned away from the window, and said calmly, "I want to be sexually secure."

I do not consciously remember thinking those words before that and it was startling to hear them — even in my own mind.

Sexually secure?

This kid does communicate — in a lot of ways — and she's a little mind boggling at times. And obviously couldn't care less about ice cream.

Aggie's blue sweater has in many ways become the child for me. When I get very tired and I/the kid has had it, I go lie down with the sweater and it helps me get centered and relaxed. It's my adult form of a security blanket like my own children had when they were little. Sometimes at night I curl up around it and go to sleep sucking my thumb.

I struggle with that though. When I'm in touch with the kid in me it feels O.K. Why the hell not? I can deal with it.

But when I'm more the grown me and think about what others would think of me being so attached to a sweater I get shaky. My ego gets threatened.

Yet if I'm really honest I admit I feel better with it. I'm more secure when I just allow it to happen and forget what others might think. Inie says the world would have fewer problems if more people could allow themselves to deal with those kinds of needs. That's probably true but it's not always easy to allow it.

Shirley understands the sweater and accepts it and that helps a lot.

I've spent a lot of time with Rob during the past two days. He's better. He looks pale and thinner but he's O.K. His emotions are raw and the holes — the old emotional wounds left inside him from the past — are ripped open and bleeding.

"Every time I get it together it falls apart on me." Tears were running down his cheeks. His voice cracked as he tried to get the emotions out. "It makes me feel like I'm never going to be able to feel

I'm worth something to other people."

We talked for a long time. I could hear him because so much of what he said was mine, too. He talked about being the youngest in his family.

"My folks would talk all the time about my older brothers. Jim was in prison and Don was in college, and they were always saying, 'Well, we had one good one and one bad one.' I felt like a blank spot on the wall."

We talked.

"You're my brother, Rob, my chosen brother". We cried.

I know he can't just go trotting into one of the agencies where we've sent our clients and ask for help. And he needs to have his ego and pride built up a little first anyway.

"It's going to be O.K., man. You're going to be alright."

I told him how much his support has meant to me as I've struggled through this last few months of therapy and pain.

"You'll maybe never know how much it's meant that I could come back to you at the office — that I knew you were there. I couldn't talk about it much — it's too painful — but you were there and I knew it. And I'm going to be here for you."

He got some things out.

"I know I need to have a lot of affection shown to me. I need to be touched and hugged. I'm glad I was with Carmen and lived with her because her mom did a lot of that for me. And finally I got so I could touch my mom. She didn't know how to respond to it but I did it anyway and now. . . ."

He still bleeds over his mother's death.

In the end I simply held him before I left.

He's going to be alright.

I know I can't do treatment with him — we're way too close — but I can be there with him. I can hold him, hug him. . . . be some eyes he can look into and regain some dignity and pride. I can talk with the people he lives with about what he needs right now. And I can accept him. I can be his sister. I can help him believe that someone sees worth in him.

I love Robert.

I was lying on my bed half asleep and had a dream/memory/
something.

I saw myself at about nine or ten years old. My mother called
to me from the bedroom.

I went just into their room and saw she was getting dressed.
She was naked from her waist up and putting on her bra. She
was talking to me about something but I wasn't listening to her
because I was uptight and I was trying not to look at her.

She said, "You're not listening to me. Look at me.

"I said, "No."

"What's the matter? Are you ashamed of me?"

The dream or whatever it was ended abruptly and I was wide
awake. My groin area felt the same way it did the other night
at Inie's and I began banging my head violently against my pillow.
It was almost as if my body was controlled by another mind. I
held on to the sweater and shoved my thumb in my mouth and
the banging stopped. I began to feel more normal as I lay there
but it was an unsettling experience.

I remember her coming into the living room like that, dress-
ing in the doorway. It would make me uncomfortable. When I
try to think about it now, it flashes past my consciousness too
fast for me to really see her. I remember it more for the feelings
of uncomfortable embarrassment I felt at the time.

I woke up this morning feeling like hands were touching my body. My heart was pounding. My hair was damp with sweat and in my mind was an image of my mother's hands. That's it. It was a picture like a flash card used to teach a child the parts of the body. Only every time I saw that image I felt a pain in my vagina which, along with my groin area, was tense and uncomfortable.

I got a good hold on the sweater as my heartbeat and breathing began to slow. Then an internal monologue began.

"What time is it? 5:15. Shit. It's more of the sexual stuff. It's Tuesday. I don't see Inie until tomorrow night. I don't want to go. If I go I'm not going to close my eyes or lie down on the floor. I'm going to sit up and talk to her."

Then the flash card and the hand image jumped up in my mind and I immediately began to slam my head against the pillow.

"I'll go see her. I have to. But I hate being out of control. I hate all this damn stuff."

A new picture appeared. I saw a small child's naked body — torso really — and the hands touching it. One hand was between the legs and the thumb of the other hand was touching the groin area. A jolt of something passed through my body.

"My god". I was so small her hands covered that much of my body!"

The monologue stopped and I was full of rage.

I saw myself in Inie's small office smashing my head against the floor, pounding with my fists yelling and kicking. It was an image with violent overtones. I was beating on one of the big pillows Inie has and I heaved it across the room with brute force. I kicked it and kicked it, opened the door and hurled it down the stairs.

I rushed down the stairs and kicked it some more. Then I was back in the fantasy at the hospital and I beat my mother with no mercy. I destroyed her. I was wild with rage.

I lay on my bed in the pale morning light, sweating as if I'd actually done those things. The kid will want to get into all this as soon as she sees Inie tomorrow night I thought. There was a disturbing certainty in knowing I'd be out of control, on the floor, lost in a child's raw fit of rage.

I hope some day it will all be over. Done.

What a way to start the day.

I think I'm at the end — or near the end — of the kid getting out the painful pieces from the past. Last night the rage came and I went over the edge right on schedule but then afterwards I experienced an enormous sense of relief. It made me laugh. I laid there on the floor and giggled and laughed for twenty minutes. I laughed so hard for awhile I cried. I had the feeling we'd reached the end — that it's over — that we've come to the bottom of all the things which have kept me nailed to my emotional past.

There was an expansion of the kid's emotions and the experience of laughing happened more than once. As time went on I could feel real joy at the relief and everything — my body included — felt looser.
"I feel goofy," I'd giggle to Inie, but I couldn't stop it any more than I could stop the tears and sobs which came before.
She patiently sat through all this new emotion, too.
"It's good," she said. "Let the kid have a little fun for a change."

God damn it.

I don't know what's gone wrong but I don't like it. How am I supposed to deal with this? These pains start in my groin and vagina and up in my stomach. My legs are tense and my groin is incredibly sensitive. My skin is wild.

"Just hold her and let her relax," said Inie.

I had already stayed home in bed holding the sweater part of the morning.

"She can't always come out just when she wants to."

"Fuck it! She does too! I can't make her go away.

I'm not going to feel this crap any longer. I think you can get bogged down in introspection. After a while it runs your life. It's what I thought about on the way home from work and going to bed last night, during the night and first thing this morning. And I still felt the pain while I was driving to work.

I hate this. I hate the kid and therapy. Most of all I hate my god damned mother for what she did.

I cannot stand being like this. My body is so hyped up — so sensitive right now — it's painful to wipe myself after I urinate. I can't stand being locked in this body. There has to be a way to end this. Nobody seems to understand that I'm in here with the kid and it's driving me crazy.

Slow down. Just slow down. There has to be a way to deal with this.

People are always saying you have to deal. What the hell does that mean? Particularly now? With this?

I swear if I knew what to do, I'd do it, but I don't know what it is that will make this go away.

I called Tina and we went out for a while. She doesn't know either.

Waking up on a sunny spring morning at Shirley and Dan's cottage on Lake Michigan.

Like the effects of higher altitude in the mountains, the change of seasons is momentarily on hold here with the trees not quite as ready to bloom and with patches of snow here and there. So being here provides not only a respite from the pressures of the outside world but a slight lapse of the relentless passage of time. It feels good to lie relaxed and have the time to think.

I feel very much at home here. This place is full of memories for me.

I hear David leave for one last run on the beach before the Air Force. And thinking how he and Dan always put the sailboat in the water together — like some rite of spring. Dave's mentioned several times how he won't get to do that this year.

Life is a tender thing which needs nurturing in order to grow and blossom with love. Dave is going to be alright. If I haven't managed to give David anything else in life, he's been allowed to be human and to have others around him who've accepted that. He can take it from here because he has people who care. He'll be alright.

People just said....
Kept saying....
"You have to do it."
But no one told me that
Getting my soul rebuilt/my heart overhauled
Would be
So painful.

No one said
There will be secrets uncovered
That even you don't know about
And that you won't be able to think them
Even after you know.

No one told me
That inch by inch,
Hour by hour,
Layer by layer —
Like an onion —
I would be peeled down
To a soft,
Tender,
Defenseless core.
A child.

I didn't know
I'd have to become
A bruised and battered
Four year old
In order to emerge

A free adult.
And certainly
No one —
Not one soul —
Said I'd have to feel her feelings
Remember her body
And be her being.
Or have the trust of the combined Indian nations
And Moses to boot.

I really didn't
Understand
That.

May, 1982

Last time with Inie, it was as if I was running without oil or body fluids — those physical/psychological liquids that make human functioning possible. I had been exhausted all week — mostly from using my energy to push down and out of consciousness my feelings about the sexual abuse. And what energy was left was used to cope with David's leaving. By the time I was with Inie, I didn't want to feel anything anymore.

But the physical feelings welled up in me and the kid part of me went crazy with desire to get them out and gone. The adult me resisted even allowing them to exist.

"It feels like a war is going on between you and the kid," Inie said.

It was a war and in the end my efforts failed. Both my body and mind stretched to a point of breaking, like some humanized rubber band. For a while I was the child again — pushed and pulled beyond where I could go. I was past the point of stimulation that I could handle and then — pow — snap — I had this childish little orgasm — high and light, little, like a small bird passing quickly through me — and then suddenly bang — there I was — an adult, exhausted, lying on my therapist's floor, fully realizing at again a deeper level, that as a small child I experienced my mother sexually. I lay there knowing she stimulated me sexually a number of ways including orally.

My mind still screams when I write those words. Orally. It's an image like the targets in shooting galleries at summer carnivals. It flashes in front of me so fast that my mind sees it and rejects it all in one movement, and the seeing causes a snapping jolt in my mind. At the bottom of this whole pile of feelings, experiences, images, and thoughts — at the farthest extent the therapy had pushed me — I can't get my mind fully connected with that piece. The idea that my mother stimulated me sexually, touched me with her hands/fingers, that I was very young, that I had orgasms as a result of that stimulation — all that — I'm getting more resolved — as much as it's resolvable. But to think about my mother touching me — with her mouth/tongue — is past where my mind can go. That thought makes my body jerk.

When I tried to think about it — when Inie said ''Do you want to talk about it?'' — I couldn't lie down anymore. I had to at least pull myself back together enough to sit up. We didn't really talk much that day. I was too drained.

''She's some kid,'' Inie said.

Times like that were extremely difficult for me. It would take days to fully recover my composure. I'd still go to work and carry on my life, but internally I'd be deeply shaken.

Through it all, it helped a great deal that Inie expressed her appreciation for the kid and for her refusal to be silenced.

''It's important that you hear her,'' Inie would say. ''She's not going to be silenced any more and she's a good girl.''

Part of my strength to hang in came from Inie's appreciation of the kid. Certainly Inie was in a better position than anyone else to see and know the kid and I went on trust that if Inie thought the kid was great then she must be worth fighting for.

Another part was the physical feelings in my body. I could not deny

what I felt or the changes that were occurring. They were too real.
  "She's some kid," Inie would say.

"How are you feeling?" asked Inie.

I try hard to be honest with her and the therapeutic process. I felt tight and my stomach hurt.

"I feel blocked," I told her. "It's like there's a big block of something in my stomach."

"Try to focus on that," she said.

The more I tried to stay with that feeling the more my stomach hurt. I remember thinking "What would the block be? What's being blocked out?" — and I thought about the oral sex and I felt nauseated. A wave of revulsion passed through me and I tried to keep from getting sick and vomiting, and suddenly it was like an emotional/physical eruption of my being. I exploded. I was on the floor yelling, twisting, kicking, pounding, banging my head and saying "No! No! No! No! No!" I could not stop. I was a rocket making its ascent, having its flight, and I could do little more than hang on for the ride.

"That's right! No! No!" I heard Inie encouraging me at one point. "No more! Tell her no more! That's right!"

Then another wave of whatever it was passed through me and I was again flailing and yelling. It went on and on and finally I was simply spent and I woke up later face down on the carpet.

"How do you feel now?" asked Inie. Relieved. I felt physically released and as if the emotional fluids were again flowing in me — as if I were not so emotionally dry. I felt less friction and tightness when I thought. I started to laugh and smile again. It felt a little silly but good, too. The week before when it happened I'd told Inie I felt sort of goofy, and that's the way it feels. I was feeling good and relieved so soon after all that and it made me laugh. I could feel the energy beginning to flow again.

My mind struggles
Desperately
With/against
This piece

My little mind has been
Bent/snapped/shredded and peeled
But I cannot get it
Wrapped around this idea
That I had—
At no matter how young/unconscious an age—
Orgasmic sex with my mother.
It does not bend that far.

Oh, I can do it.
At some surface level
I can think and say
"I don't like it but it happened."
Or I can do some nifty psychological gyrations and say
"It was like in a different lifetime/ someone else."
But to just sit down and get
A good firm grip on it....
I can't.

Today was hell —
Filled with physical feelings
Pushing me hard against the reality wall
Saying....It was you....It was your body/your mother.
And in response/exhaustion
My mind has simply turned
Away
And into melting grape jelly.

My therapist says "Let the kid tell you."
Tell me?!
The kid is driving me nuts.

I struggle to get hold of this —
Understand it—
And the kid
Throws old images and feelings at me
Like I'm some god damned dart board
And then leaves me
On my emotional knees.

"Hold her. The kid is scared."
Says the calm voice on the telephone.
"She needs to be reassured."
She needs it?!
She should learn the old do unto others trick.
She's as reassuring as a crazed bear.

Screw it.
What's the point anyway?
Will there come a time when I can
Without the slightest flinching say
"It's done. It doesn't matter anymore."
Or will I simply
Have less pain and focus on the past?

Perhaps if I am lucky I will be able
To think about how, at one point,
I had sex/orgasms
With my own mother —
And not get sick in my stomach at the thought.

So what the hell kind of goal is that?
To not get sick when my own mind works?
I'm spending this amount of energy
For that?
It seems like there ought to be
Some simple human rights

Which allows us all to have
Higher goals in life.

"Hang in there.
It's important that you work it through."
Yeah? That's easy for you to say.

Resolution.
It's called resolution.

Fuck.
Fuck it.
Fuck it all, man.
Because I don't give a damn
What anybody says—
If you try
To bend your mind that far,
It disturbs your guts
Which lie right next
To where the soul is housed
In any human body that's been
Screwed by its mother.
And then all night long
There are screams in the dark
Saying
"Mama, don't."
Because you want to be loved/held
For the child you are/were.
And it really doesn't matter how old you are.
That's the way it is.

4/24/82

Last week with Inie I think I said out loud what the kid says inside me all the time.

"I don't care! It's dumb! I don't need anybody!"
(Only if I'm really upset the kid also says "Leave me alone!")

Inie told me later that may have been how the kid coped but it's no longer an appropriate response. That's true, but it's very real and I don't know how else to respond.

I allow myself to feel that need with only a few trusted people and if something goes wrong my self concept is such that I don't feel there are lots of other options. And then I don't feel — especially when my confidence is shaken — very lovable/attractive/acceptable/grown-up or wanted. It is far better to not need or even feel the need to be held.

At any rate, I've had little experience in life which predisposes me towards comfort when I'm touched, to feel the need for touching, or have feelings which might lead me to sexual intimacy. That entire continuum is threatening. And the other night left me deeply shaken.

I felt shaken partly because I felt those feelings while I was with a woman. I've said I don't think they were as directed towards Inie as simply felt in her presence. And I've talked with her about how naive I feel about my sexuality as related to other women. It scares me a little that I felt that with her. On the other hand I'm enough of a feminist that it seems dumb to get uptight. If I'd felt that in the presence of a male therapist, would it have been more acceptable? And I don't think the kid is real selective about who it happens with. But in all honesty the adult me will get uptight if it happens with someone other than Inie.

I think Inie and I both feel maybe this process is going to end soon. Not totally end, but the process as it is now is going to change.

The unearthing of all the buried things from the past is nearly complete. Nothing else seems to be pushing for release. And now I need to look at some other agenda items. I've had little energy to explore who I can become.

And the kid part of me needs time to grow and feel nurtured. She's now been through all this twice and simply needs to be herself and play — be a kid for a while. She's getting better — more secure. For a while I sucked my thumb a remarkable amount of time — every night when I went to sleep, during the night, when I woke up in the morning, and if I was really stressed at other times I'd lie down and do it for a while. Once I went home for lunch to do it. But now it's becoming more for simple pleasure or comfort and less in desperation.

I still sleep with Aggie's blue sweater. I even took it to therapy one night. But I think I did that partly because somehow the child is slowly slipping out of it. For a long time I had to hold it tightly in order to go to sleep — as much of it had to touch me as possible. Now I'm a little surprised to sometimes wake up and find it out of my arms — even if it's only a few inches away. I think I took it to Inie's that night to have her see it before it grew up — the way one woman might want another to see her baby while it's still a baby.

"It's good you brought it," Inie said. "It's like it represents the child but it's a comfort to you all at the same time."

That's true. And now I'm not needing such gross amounts of comfort. Before I'd felt pushed emotionally — knowing something was forcing its way up and out of me. And that session I felt the sexual abuse in a new way — at a new level. I remember crying and saying something like "She hurt my baby." I don't remember ever thinking of the sweater as "my baby" before then. I think I experienced at a new level of awareness that "my baby"/I the baby, had been terribly hurt.

I asked Inie "Do you want to hold it?" I was putting my shoes back on and Inie held the sweater while I did that. I said it sort of as a joke.

Since that time I've thought I'd like to take the sweater back and ask her to hold it before the child/baby slips out of it for me. If all I have left — all that perhaps is left — of her is the feelings I have invested in this sweater, then no matter how farfetched it may seem, I'd like/need to see "her" held. I need to see/feel her cuddled and comforted, rocked a little and handled gently. I think I need to risk physically handing the emotions the sweater represents over to another human being and trusting that action and the response it will get. I need to let go of what was and allow something else to take its place. Most of all I need to allow myself and the kid to feel those emotions and not feel sexually threatened or used while they're felt. I need to feel those feelings and needs and yet feel safe all at the same time. Maybe this sounds crazy — I don't know. But in my guts I think I need to have that basic human contact.

I have the feeling growing in me that at some point down the road I will be able to leave therapy and cope with my own self again. But I would like to take with me an emotional/mental picture or snapshot of my child finally being held like a child. Then I'd be able to take that out and look at it and know that for everything else that happened, I had that, too.

Dear Inie,
Please hold my child. I/she needs it. Take her in your arms and hold her next to you as if there is value in her just because she's a human being. She already trusts you a lot because for all the times you've touched her and she's/I've been vulnerable with you, you've never betrayed her. She/I know you will not take advantage of her need.

There are terrible holes in the kid. Some are needs that were never filled and some are wounds from what was. My child loves you because you didn't embarrass her because of her condition and because you've cared enough to fill so many of the holes. You've healed much of her pain and I am grateful.

I don't know if I can ever really give you anything or say anything which will tell you how you've helped. I am becoming — slowly, painfully, remarkably — the kid. The distance is getting less each week. Before I lose the sense of her as a separate, little human being, please hold her — physically — for a while. We both need it.
Love,
Kathy

I got scared about what I'd written last time about asking Inie to hold the sweater and when I got with her I began to feel uncomfortable and vulnerable. Driving over there I thought I must be getting crazy. There I was taking a sweater to someone to ask them to hold it like it was a baby or small child. Yet when I had gotten in touch with those feelings and my desire to have Inie hold the sweater, it had been an encounter with something very real. I had cried as I wrote those words, and it took me hours to do it.

But when it came to actually sharing those with her, to read, I felt panic. Sitting while she read them was agony. Part of me was saying "My god! You're forty years old and asking someone to hold a sweater you sleep with because sometimes it feels like the baby/child you were a long time ago, but now you think the sweater may be growing up!" Another voice in me was saying "Trust your feeling and the process. Trust Inie. Trust yourself."

I was so involved in that internal struggle and with clutching the sweater that when Inie finished reading and touched me I was startled. She slowly reached out and pulled me into her arms. "Come on, we'll hold her together," she said. As she did that I began to sob. Something was passing up and out of the core of my being and it was a relief to be held — to feel safe. I clutched the sweater to me and felt very young and small as she rocked me.

After a while I felt spent/done and I leaned back in the chair. I felt emotionally emptied. It was as if there was nothing left.

But then Inie slowly/calmly took the sweater from my arms. Part of me was screaming "No! No!" but another part was saying "Yes, please hold her." It caused a terrible moment of panic — the kind of fear animals show when someone else gets near their young.

Seeing her actually hold it — to see her take it against her body, cuddle it like a newborn as if it's head had been placed gently on her shoulder, seeing her place her cheek against it and stroke it softly — was more than I could handle. I wept as if the tears were coming from the heart of the little person I must have been. It felt overwhelming to see. And I'm not sure I fully understand it all yet.

"I think you've made it — the kid's made it," Inie said. "I think you and the kid are one person now."

I hope that's true. I hope I/the split is healed. It's crazy but I think that's true. For so long I guess I was split and didn't know it and now I've gone through this intense period of knowing and feeling that split. Now if I'm whole I don't know exactly what to expect. Maybe that becomes clearer with time.

We talked about other things, too. I struggled to try to explain to her that I can't make a very clear/tight connection in my mind with the whole experience of oral sex in my childhood.

"It's like a formula that says I know it happened because physical feelings A and B are so real. But I can't get a tight grip on any of the parts of the formula or on all of them at once."

We talked about that and decided that maybe that's because it all happened when I was so young — before I had the capacity to make those mental connections. There was some relief in understanding that maybe that's the block.

I told her I thought when I first came to see her the child was about ten and wanted to sit on the floor and feel Inie bigger and stronger while she sat in her chair above me. Then the kid was about four or five through most of the therapy. She does not like going into Inie's office alone and she has little patience. But there were times when the kid was just a baby — especially as related to the oral sex experience. Now the kid feels about six and there is a sense that she is growing up. We've turned some corner and she's growing up now. At the same time, interestingly enough, I also sense that she is becoming more me and I am becoming more her. I don't know how to explain that but that's how it feels.

Inie held me again before I left and then she took the sweater into her arms as if it were her first grandchild. It was a very emotional experience for me again.

"What does it feel like when you hold it?" I asked as I again settled down.

Hearing her answer I realized what I really wanted to know was, does it feel good to you?

"Yes," she said.

Suddenly it was like a mischievous kid overwhelmed me and I said "Do you want to suck your thumb?"

We both laughed very hard. It presented such a ridiculous picture and I was laughing at myself. I have spent months sucking mine.

3:00 A.M.

I presented an award in memory of Aggie tonight.

One more time I managed to talk publicly about her — about losing her — without coming totally undone. And I'm glad I did it. Several people came afterwards and thanked me for it.

Looking back, being in touch with all those feelings again, I think I recognize now I was emotionally/critically wounded when she died. Surely if there were fluids which nourished and sustained people emotionally I was — for weeks — lying near death in a pool of those fluids. They were leaking from my spirit and I couldn't stop them. Thank god some friends picked me up and put me in therapy.

A young police officer who nearly died in a terrible shooting last year, also was honored. I was very deeply touched that she was there — alive.

The Lord giveth and the Lord taketh away and all that jazz. I know, I know. But god I still miss Aggie.

There's a funny little thing that happens.
Sometimes when I lay down—
Settling in for the night.
Ready to turn off the outside/adult world—
I say
"Mama?"

It's like a half question/half statement
And I never really know what it means.
When I say it I'm usually rocking the sweater against me
As if to comfort it or wake it up.

"Mama?"

Maybe it's the child in me
Asking an old question:
Who is this who enters my space?
Who's putting their body next to me?
What can I expect?

I wonder if
When I was little
I really asked that?
Did "Mama?" mean
"Who is it in the dark?
Are you the one who
Gently touched my face
And whose hands I remember?
Or are you the one who touched me elsewhere
And whose hands I try to forget?"

And I always say it in a little voice—
 Not baby talk—
But a small, tentative voice.
Cautious.
But I can't get it connected
To any other words,

**There are no thoughts to explain or expand it—,
Just "Mama?"**

---

*I had an unending desire for the therapy to move and be complete. I
hated going, and week after week, would write things like the following.*

I think I've gone as far as I can go with this. For a long time it
felt — even though I really didn't understand it — there was a sense
of direction/movement. The "process" was going somewhere.
Now it feels like a sailboat caught in the irons—that condition on
the water when there isn't enough breeze to move the boat no matter which angle you get the sail. You can't catch the wind. You just
sit there waiting for some action to occur and it can get very trying. I've never liked therapy much but it at least felt like there was
a creative/moving tension happening. Now it's just trying.

---

*These complaints would be included in the same material as descrip-
tions of weeks when I had an orgasm in the middle of a session, a new
memory surfaced, or any variety of other major developments occurred.
Looking back at these passages now I think they were actually my deeply
ingrained denial of what was happening, of what I was faced with in the
therapy, and my desire to be done. I grew to love and respect Inie, but
I never loved the therapy.*

Somehow it doesn't feel quite honest anymore. I'm not real comfortable with the focus on the sexual stuff. I'm not sure I understand everything related to my sexuality or sex in general or that

I know how to talk about it very well. It seems hard to even stay focused on it. There is less "work" during the week between sessions and I'm not sure if that's because the whole process is winding down or I can't focus on what we've talked about.

I know last time with Inie I got very scared. I wonder if we need to talk about if my early experiences have left me uptight about feeling sexual in the presence of women. The other day I remembered something which happened with Tina a few years ago which made me uncomfortable.

We were in an apartment, had both flopped on a bed while we waited for Shirley, and were simply talking. I don't remember what we were talking about now but it was something general and non-sexual like jobs or whatever. And I suddenly wondered what it would feel like to kiss her. When I realized what I was thinking I must have had the same look on my face that I had with Inie because Tina said "Take it easy. It's alright." But I was uncomfortable.

Nothing sexual happened. We talked about it. Tina loves to feel like she's helping me out in such matters. But I'd forgotten all about it until the other day.

Tina and I have slept together several times since then and before that occurrence. We touch each other and have been naked together while changing clothes, going to the spa, etc. Nothing has ever happened, but that incident is like a novel in Greek to me. I don't understand it.

Do you feel sexual or have sexual thoughts only about and because of the person you're with or do they just happen. . . . sort of freestyle. . . . and you happen to be with someone at the time? I feel dumb writing this. . . .very juvenile. . . .but I really don't know. I think I've blocked it out so much of the time that I don't know about that from experience. And do other women feel that or think that? If I feel it in the presence of women does that make me bisexual? I don't mean I need a label for everything but I really don't understand. And it's painful to be so naive.

I suppose I need to talk about all this but I'm not sure how or even what to talk about. How do you know what other women feel? Maybe I'm normal. Do you ask someone like Geri to lunch and say "By the way, do you ever. . . .?" Or how about "A funny thing happened to me over at Inie's the other night. Have you ever. . . .?" It all feels uncomfortable and I wish I'd done all this at twelve.

And going out and doing a lot of experimenting isn't exactly my style either. That's just not my style.

When I try to focus on sex and how I feel about it I feel dumb.

The other night I told Inie about a guy I find attractive. I felt fourteen talking about it.

God. What a case of arrested development.

I wrote to David and told him about the therapy, the abuse, and sent him a copy of the article from last winter. I wrote and mailed it within a couple of hours. I'm not sure why I did it.

I told him I know that she was his grandmother, but that she was sick when I was little, and I know that she may have been a very different person in his life. But I need to deal with it for me no matter who she was to other people. I said I didn't want to spoil anything for him — his memories or feelings — but I also wanted him to know.

This is probably a lousy time to tell him about it, but there is no good time, and I needed to tell someone in my family, I think.

After that I called the Women's Resource Center to find out when the incest support groups meet. Their rule is you have to talk to someone on the phone before you are assigned to a group. I just want to go, listen, and see if I want to be a part of it. Someone's going to call me back. I think I already know I'm going to tell who ever calls that I was calling for a client who was interested but she's changed her mind. Thanks anyway. Goodbye.

I'm not going to talk about that to some voice that I don't even know.

Period.

No.

I feel sort of down. Depressed. Confused. Anxious. I feel alone.

Dumb. How the hell long can my condition of helplessness persist?

How long can a person be such a simp?

I don't think I want to go to therapy anymore.

I talked on the phone to a young woman named Laurie who called about the incest support groups. She said she remembered me from the evening I presented Aggie's award. (That made me uncomfortable.)

She told me about the groups and as she spoke I could hear a tightness in her voice grow and I realized it was a risk for her to call me about this, too. I could hear the sounds of myself as she spoke of her own experiences.

After awhile she asked the magic question.

"Are you calling for yourself?"

It was hard to say yes. First I said I had clients who are dealing with it, which is true. I guess that bought me fifteen more seconds of denial. Then I said I was calling for myself, too. I guess I probably said it the way I talked with Inie the first time. Stand tall. Be brave.

But once that barrier was crossed — once we had both said it had happened — I was astounded at all we talked about in the next hour and a half. I think we could both feel heard and it was easy to see that we were both struggling with some of the same issues.

Yet when we turned back to the question of the groups, it was still hard to think about going and talking about the same things in a group. I'm not sure I'm ready for that. Maybe I can just talk to Laurie a couple of times before I go to the group.

I am not going to push this any faster than it will go.

This is a difficult period. I'm struggling to stay with the therapy, the agenda and Inie. It's been hard for me to focus on it all and to write about it. There's a tight, dry tension attached to all this and it feels like it's off the tracks.

I had a dream which I did not record and had pretty much dismissed. But then I told it to Inie and as she verbally explored it I became upset and angry.

In the dream I was in another country/culture — probably Mexico — living in a small village. It was dry and warm, nearly dark, and there was an approaching storm. I was going to the store, carrying Aggie's sweater as if it were a baby, and I was dressed in a cotton blouse and skirt with sandals.

This seemed a poor village and the only lights were in the store. There were a few people gathered at the store as if getting things before the storm and darkness arrived. There was a sense of urgency and it was beginning to sprinkle. On the sidewalk, in the light from the window, was a small boy lying on his stomach. He was about two or three years old, brown, had dark, curly hair, and was dressed only in shorts. People were either moving past him without looking or ignoring him as they stood talking near him. I had seen this child before and was concerned about what would happen to him during the storm. I asked some nearby men about him and they said not to worry about him since he was a beggar — a wild boy — who took care of himself. He would be alright they said.

I then looked at the sweater in my arms and it turned into a child — me as a child — and when I looked at the boy again I realized they looked alike — as if they were brother and sister and the same age.

That was all I could remember from the dream. When Inie talked about the dream she said that the boy was a part of me, and that in this culture little boys in dreams often symbolize the part of us that is active and can do things. She said perhaps it was also the part of me that was neglected as a child.

I began to feel uncomfortable as she spoke about all this, and the emotion began to rise in me. I struggled with all the feelings in me and became so tired I needed to lie down on the floor. As I relaxed I began to tell her about how when I was small I tried to stay out of the house and away from my family. I spent a lot of time in the woods and fields by myself. The way that was seen and explained by my family and the neighbors was that ''that's the Indian in her.'' As I told that to Inie I became furious at what a rotten trick that was to play on a kid. What a handy way to hide the effects of the abuse I'd experienced. Saying it to Inie made me enraged and I was soon kicking the floor and cursing them all.

I was astounded by the potency of that little dream. It felt like it came out of left field and shook my confidence in believing I have any idea of where I am in this process. I'd thought that might be the last night. . . .that there was little left to examine and I'd skip the next appointment. Instead I felt shaken by what I'd not known was even there.

"Are there two children," I asked Inie.

"No. It's part of the same child in you which is you."

Nonetheless, now there is this image of a small boy child lying on a dusty Mexican sidewalk and it sort of hangs in a corner of my mind. Inie asked if the boy was inside me and I don't know. I think he's still asleep there and it feels unsettled.

From time to time the focus of the therapy/process would shift to the relationship between Inie and I and that was often difficult for me.

It seems to have shaken the process that Inie did not read the material I'd written while I was there last week. I had risked some things in writing before I could verbalize them and I had written about myself and my sexuality. I guess that was a bigger risk than I realized. By the time that material had been held over a week I was more than uneasy. Sometimes I'm uncomfortable while she reads the writing in my presence but this time I was up tight that she hadn't. When I arrived by the following week knowing she'd probably read it by then I felt like I'd left a loaded gun with her.

Soon after I got there she leaned forward slightly in her chair and began to carefully bring up the writing from last week.

"You know, you wrote last week about — and — , and I don't want to set the agenda, but maybe we should talk about that. But I don't want to set the agenda."

When two people try to talk and one feels the other has a weapon, that becomes the agenda.

I tried to say "It feels like this process has peeled off layer after layer of me and now I'm down to a soft, defenseless core. Part of that vulnerable core is my sexual identity and it feels like that's coming unglued. I feel very scared and vulnerable, and feel you're much stronger than I am."

Somehow it felt like Inie heard, "You put me through this process which has peeled me down to a vulnerable core and you're stronger than I am."

Suddenly we seemed off in the direction of her saying "It's your process, you've peeled yourself, and I don't have any real power in this. You do."

My adult, gut reaction to that was, "Bullshit. Don't tell me things aren't unbalanced when it's my sexuality/sexual identity that becomes the topic of discussion and not yours. Let me read what you have to say about that part of yourself, give me a week to think about it, and we'll settle in for a couple of hours of probing your insides."

And if the adult me was having problems, the kid was going nuts. At her very best, in a sexual sense, I think the kid is twelve years old. I'm not sure the kid is ready for dealing with this. And once the kid falls apart the balance in the relationship between Inie and me is gone, no matter what words are used to say it isn't.

What I think could have helped at that point was for Inie to say something like "It's O.K. Relax. No one's going to push you to talk about it or do anything about it, but if you want to talk, we will. And if we do, you can stop anytime you want to and rest/think a while. And no one — not even me, has the right to push you in one direction or the other sexually — especially while you feel so vulnerable. I'll stay with you and you can take your time if you need to, and you'll be safe here with me."

Maybe she tried to say those things and I couldn't hear her. I have heard her say "Things are different now. You don't have to do anything you don't want to do."

My internal reaction is "Do anything? God, I can't even talk about it yet, let alone do anything!"

She has said "It won't matter if it's a man or a woman or who it is as long as you're honest." But just saying it feels like pressure.

The sequence of this process for me has repeatedly been to get connected with the fact that an issue exists, think about it, write about it, talk about it, and then maybe do it or think more. This is not an agenda item which can be pushed. I know I need to talk about it, and I think I will, but I need some time and space, and for Inie to be gentle with the process.

The kid in me feels very young and not at all sure what to do. Sometimes I feel like I'm really going out into the world for the first time.

In truth, I'd find it difficult if right now someone approached me with a message which said essentially "I find you sexually attractive and would like to get to know that part of you." The kid may be curious, but she's not ready for anything more than curiosity right now. She/I need the chance to talk all this through and not feel pushed or forced.

It was a relief when I talked with Laurie about the incest. So many things she said made me feel that she knew what I'd been through. When we'd talked on the phone she'd mentioned three different groups, and the Women's Resource Center had told me there were two.

"You'll be in the Monday night group with me," she'd said.

Afterwards I kept thinking, "What Monday night group?" Someone had told me they had a friend in a lesbian incest support group. I kept wondering if that was the Monday night group Laurie had mentioned. Try as I might, the very idea would make panic rise in me. God, I'm not ready for that, I kept thinking. I called Laurie back.

"Hi," I said bravely. "Ah....I'd like to get together with you before I go to the group for the first time. I think that would really help me."

It was true. But I actually wanted to know more about the group. It turned out to be an excellent move.

Laurie is young — about thirty — and was very open to talking.

I told her I did not want to be under a huge amount of pressure — that I had lots of it with my job. Telling others about my incest experiences and listening to them would be a lot added on, and I felt strange enough that my experience was with my mother. I felt scared to make the move to enter a group where sex and sexuality was an open agenda item. And I managed to ask her about my concerns about who was in the group.

As it turned out, it is not strictly a lesbian group, but there are lesbians in the group. I think after talking with Laurie that could be a healthy thing for me.

I feel less vulnerable now because I was able to focus on my concerns and talk them through. It was a positive experience to have Laurie just accept them. This may sound like an exercise in flakiness, but it's the first time I've been able to verbalize some concern related to sex and feel like it's gotten resolved or really heard. It feels positive to me even if it sounds stupid to someone else.

I think I need to go through the process of turning the voltage down by saying I'm going to do this at my own speed and at a manageable level of intensity. I think that can be done with Inie, the journal, and maybe the support group.

I need to get this mess sorted out. Right now all this feels like scrambled emotions stored under a broad category labelled ''sex and sexuality''. Everything that's been too much to deal with has just been thrown in that file.

As I worked through things with Laurie, there was the dawning realization that I have felt pressure around my sexuality for a long time. Getting in touch with the incest has certainly made it easier to understand the pressure. And being peeled down to the basics of my sexual identity and feeling emotionally naked as I do is really probably a tremendous opportunity to be more settled. And I think it would be real helpful to me as a counsellor if I can struggle through that.

More and more in the time with Inie there was increased time spent with the kid subdued and my adult being able to talk with Inie — less time spent on "the level where the kid is" as Inie described it. Less with me "out to lunch" as I called it.

However, that seemed to bring new issues for us.

My relationship with Inie has been remarkably productive and helpful, while at the same time it feels enormously out of balance, to the extent that there are times when I can barely stand to remain in the relationship at all. The process of the therapy has been like one of those trick foreground/background pictures and I can't get it straight, I guess. The stuff with the kid has been so intense that I've focused on that, and the relationship with Inie has been in the background.

It took real effort to maintain such an intense relationship, and while she's a remarkably calm and steady person, I knew it had to be a struggle for her, too, at times.

I went to the incest support group for the first time, and there were seven other women there. Some have been in the group for as long as two years.

Besides Laurie, there was a registered nurse, a farm wife, a young, unmarried mother, a social worker, a factory worker, and a woman about to leave the group to start another one in the community where she lives. They were a little ragged getting started, but were very serious about the process once they did.

I just listened quietly to what was being said by others, and it was often painful to hear others verbalize thoughts and feelings I'd had. It was like having my own reality put right in my face. I was exhausted when I got home.

The next morning I had breakfast with Shirley and our old tennis group. And afterwards Shirley and I talked for a long time.

It felt like there were a dozen topics to talk about at once: the group, my need to figure out my future, the therapy, going to school, quitting my job, getting a divorce, men, etc., all in my head at once.

She was great and we talked through the entire pile, which was, I think, a reaction to going to the incest group. Maybe by listening to others I could see the impact of my own experience, and that in a way I'm a "recovering person." While my experience and feelings are unique results of that experience, they are also common, in that I can hear myself in others in the group. Their words are also my thoughts and feelings. Their voices are mine. Their emotional movements tap into my own.

The second night in the group I still could not say I needed time to talk about a personal issue or feeling. Having worked with groups a lot, however, I also know that when one member does not conform to the unspoken rules about self disclosure, there is stress for others from not knowing the silent member. But I could not say I needed to be the focus and express myself. I can talk in the group, respond, add input, etc., but when the question was asked "Who needs time tonight?" I couldn't put the focus on me.

It's clear there are leftover effects which, unless they're consciously recognized and handled, can control aspects of our lives while we are totally unaware of it. For example, one woman talked about her difficulty in being touched and the problems that creates when, even if she initiates the touching, the response is more that she can deal with.

"I want to touch him and show him I care," she said. "but he always wants more. If I kiss his cheek, he wants to kiss my lips. If I hug him, he wants to lie down. If I lie down, he wants to have sex. If I stay with him one night, he wants two. I just can't stand it. I feel like I'll suffocate."

"How does that connect with the past . . . the incest?" someone asks, and forces the connection.

Another woman said she'd hoped to feel better/resolved after she talked with her brother who'd molested her.

"But I don't," she said.

The group helped her to feel comfortable with that realization for now.

One person talked about her fear of going to the bathroom. She shared her leftover fantasy of tiny men in the toilet who want to shoot her in the vagina when she takes down her panties. Needless to say it makes things difficult. Others supported her by sharing their own problems with bathrooms and feeling vulnerable.

There seems to be tremendous problems with self esteem and trust and being able to receive positive messages, a problem against which they know they have to struggle.

"I can hear that about anyone except myself," said one of the stronger members of the group of a positive statement about herself.

And the description of the actual incest experience . . . . the words used by one member to tell something she'd remembered and needed to talk about . . . . were almost too much for me to hear.

". . . and he put his finger in my rectum and wiggled it around while I was lying scrunched up on my face and chest."

One member of the group said she wanted me to know she was a lesbian. She said she needed to know how I would be with that, because if she was going to have the freedom in the group to work on her own real problems with sexuality, she needed to know she wouldn't be rejected by me for who she is.

"I have some real struggles with the stereotypes," she said. "If I talk to some people about having been raped by my father they seem to think 'Oh, that's why you're a lesbian.' And that's not true. I'm a lesbian. I didn't choose that, I am that. And when I was young, my father raped me. Period. Anyway, I need to know you can deal with who I am."

Looking at her soft young face and recognizing her need for basic human acceptance — a need not unlike my own — I felt a little ashamed of my fears before I came to the group.

Another member of the group said it was difficult for her that she'd introduced herself to me as not only a victim but a perpetrator. She was needing to refocus on her experience with her son, saying my being in the group had forced that, and was concerned about what I thought. She felt vulnerable because I'd been abused by my mother, and even though I had not connected her to my experiences in any way, and I felt positive towards her, and could hear her fear, it was difficult for her to get any positive messages from me. That block in her made me uncomfortable.

I think it's remarkable that she can admit it, that she's talked to her son about it, and that she can express her remorse. I guess I can understand that she feels badly, but I can't quite get connected with why she needs to hold so tightly to the idea that she's a terrible person. I doubt there's a sensitive parent alive who can't look back and say I should have done that differently, or better, or not at all. And yes, I agree, it was "a terrible thing to do to another person," but it's done, and this woman has done everything she can to resolve it and is now helping others. For her to continue to put herself down and attack her own self esteem because of her past is wrong. The struggle is in the direction of what's normal, healthy, and positive in life, and I think to get there, we have to let go and experience what it feels like to stand on our own two feet emotionally without the imbalance this bag of old crap makes when it's thrown over our back and dragged along. It seems like one element of freedom is to accept being free.

The language of all this is interesting. To be an "incest survivor" as opposed to being an "incest victim" is probably a critical mind set. To feel like a victim seems to say it's a more permanent condition like slavery or having a disease. To be a survivor, to my mind anyway, means more it was an experience one can pass through and recover from. It makes me think of Abraham Maslow and his question, ''And what shall we think of the well-adjusted slave?''

I do not want to be a well-adjusted victim, and therefore I believe I need to participate in my own emotional emancipation. I need to choose to be free from the effects of the incest to the greatest possible extent I can achieve. I don't mean I can suddenly ignore the impact of all this and just walk away from it as though I grew up in wonderland. I mean I can choose to allow it to have a minimum negative impact by facing it and moving on.

In short, I guess you scale it down to size and deal with it the same way you have to face and cope with life's other tragedies and wrong turns. You make it fit on to the list of all the other human potentials like love and war and suicide and tenderness. You have to allow other people and yourself to be human and to struggle to become what you can be, and more than we've all been.

I don't know how else to do it.

I am going on —
Out where the big kids play and are —
Where life is
Bumps and knocks,
Touches and caresses,
Laughter and tears —
I'm going on.

Sometimes I'm scared —
Afraid of what's out there/
Who I am
But sometimes too
I know
It's really just
The apprehension/anticipation
Of my twelve year old kid.
She's curious.
She wants to know
What life is all about.

Other times there is
A slightly nervous,
Excited laughter which
Bubbles up through me
And makes me smile —
About something I don't even know yet.
I am going on.
I am. . . .
I am: entering junior high school,
          seeing mountains for the first time,
          waiting for the race to begin,
          seeing a baby born,
          completing a huge, difficult task,
          barefoot on the first warm day of spring,
          riding a bike for the first time at five,
          and making my own music.

I am going on.

ONE YEAR LATER

Looking back
I have to say that
Most of all I'm grateful

I am grateful that during those mean and painful months
There were
Friends—
With kind words and gentle, supportive touches.
People—
Whose eyes told me how deeply they cared.
And I'm grateful for those who —
Without knowing of my pain, for I could not speak of it
too often,
Simply continued to be my friend—
Laughed and played with me—
And gave my life moments of joy and friendship.
And who through their unknowing gave me space
To rest from the struggle.

I am grateful for the group I joined.
Grateful that there were others—
Women —
Who spoke,
Who said it does happen. That it had happened to them.
Their courage and bravery gave me enormous support. And
I am grateful that I am no longer alone.
My painful separateness from the rest of humanity
Ceased to exist with them.

But most of all I want to say—
Need to say—

I am grateful for her. . . .
For Inie's investment in me.

I went to her in agony—
Emotionally bent from the weight of pain
and she simply said
"I can perhaps act as midwife—
I can support and help in some ways—
But the process has to be yours."

And so I set forth
On an enormously physical/intense process
In which I screamed,
Cried,
Kicked,
Banged my head on her floor,
Got carpet burns,
Stuttered,
Trembled,
And was at times terrified.

"You can do it.
"You can face these things," she said.

And I was
Held,
Rocked,
Stroked
And valued.
And somehow together
We got there.
We arrived at a point where I—
My child—
Was born/reborn.

And from there I started back in the direction

of living/Choosing to live again.

"It was your process.
You did it," she will say now.

But it's important for me to say
That while that's true—
It's also true that even on that first day with her—
,During those first hours so long ago—
,I felt someone older, stronger, and wiser
Take up a place behind me
and gently place two firm hands on my shoulders.
She steadied me through the most dangerous passage
of my life
And helped me feel I did not have to balance/save
myself alone.

While that passage/the process
Is done in many ways,
Those hands/that firm relationship
Still exists.
And now I feel she is my friend.
Simple as that.
And for that I am deeply grateful.

     1982

AFTERWORD

Looking back over these writings and rethinking the process of my treatment and incest experience there are a few thoughts I'd like to share in closing. And I'd like you to know the outcomes for some others also.

My friend Shirley is now an attorney and doing well.

Robert is good. We're working together again and daily I can see his recovery process blossom and grow. He's getting stronger and more calmly centered in a healthier sense of himself and it makes my heart glad to see it. He and Sherry have two beautiful, happy kids and we spend a lot of family time together. Being with them and their kids is a real comfort in my life.

After my mother died, my dad pushed me away and it's felt painfully rejecting. I hadn't expected that. I think it's all tied to the old family business and secrets. He married again very soon and it's as if he wants to leave a lot of his old life behind, and that includes me. So I haven't talked to anyone in my family about the incest yet, and probably won't. I have chosen to put the distance there. I've found that I not only need to be free of the effects of the abuse, but that there was a lot of accompanying craziness that I need to be free of as well.

I've become good friends with Laurie from the incest support group. We've been good for each other. Spending time with another survivor, talking, and feeling understood has moved us both along. Seeing her shake the effects of her past has been like seeing a butterfly find its wings and learn to fly. This week Laurie started medical school, which is something she couldn't make happen before, when she was caught in her old web. It makes me proud.

Another anniversary of Aggie's death is almost here. In a way, the pain I felt when she died was what helped me finally get to the incest, and that's been a real gift. I think she would be proud of me this year and that feels good.

There are others, too, who've helped — Ellen, Sue, and Geri are still around and supportive. There are others who could not face it, who backed away, and I could not deal with that very well, so I backed off, too. But there are new people who have come into my life for whom I'm grateful.

But when I think about this process most of all there's Inie.

She has been central to a lot of the changes in my life, where I am today, and certainly in this writing.

Looking back, it's clear Inie re-parented my kid. She held, disciplined, loved and believed in her. For that the kid simply loves her back. All that caused enormous healing, but still the kid needs the comfort of that relationship, and I/we still go see Inie as a client from time to time.

Our adult to adult relationship has also grown, and — as a therapist myself — I have great respect for Inie's skills and knowledge. She has taught me much and I consult with her on some cases.

She took some enormous risks in the way she treated me, and broke most of the rules along the way. It took guts to do that week after week, and I respect her for it.

But also I think of her wonderful, full laugh and her willingness to be real and let me know her, too. That helped a whole lot.

I suspect we'll always be in contact and deal with the fact that — as Inie describes it — ''we've been through some really important things together that can't just be turned off.'' The kid does not think about how if you do reparenting, there's a real bonding that occurs. The kid just loves Inie and expects to see her occasionally.

The adult me loves Inie also, and I know she loves me, too.

Recently I had a five year old kid referred to me for assessment. Within a few minutes she silently drew one of the most sexually explicit pictures you can imagine. My kid handled that pretty well until later, when the police officer who interviewed this child said she was just uncoordinated.

I soon found myself back on Inie's couch banging my head and screaming "I tried to tell them! I tried! I tried!" My rule of thumb has become to "keep myself emotionally clean" if I'm going to work with such cases. When I start feeling messy, it's time to call Inie and clean myself out.

Recently at a party I talked to a professional woman about child abuse. We were sitting on a deck looking out into a beautiful green woods. She works at a diagnostic center for children, and said they, too, were swamped with sexual abuse cases. In the course of our conversation she shared one of the inside staff jokes from her office.

"Some of the rural areas are really hidden pockets of it," she said. "It's incredible. It's gotten so now even the doctors at the center will recognize kids from those areas by their genetic defects before they even see their addresses. They'll say, where's this kid from? ————?"

The area she mentioned is where I grew up. "And it's the old families up there. They've been doing it for years."

It was a nice party and I'm glad I went, but I've thought mostly about her statement since.

Genetic defects?!

God. No wonder my kid couldn't make people deal with her. No wonder no one would look.

Once again it was like when the eye doctor drops one more lens in front of your eyes and says, "How do you see now?" Suddenly I could see a lot more clearly.

Slowly but slowly, I heal and understand more. I don't always like what I learn, but I understand more. A lot more.

And that all takes time. I've been telling Laurie all along when she talks about becoming a doctor, that the way you eat an elephant is one bite at a time. And it's true for this stuff, too. It takes time to digest that which is psychologically indigestible. Personally experienced pathology is not exactly milk and cookies.

And after a while, because there's so much abuse being reported now, you feel like you'll drown in it — be overwhelmed by the TV, newspapers, and others you hear about. The daycare stories make me nauseous. Sometimes I feel like it's everywhere. Once you look at it — really look — you may see the signs in a lot of places, and at the same time, feel you will never turn your back again.

After a lot of thinking, I found myself wondering about my own daughter's difficult adolescence. Why did Kerry have such a harder time than David, I kept asking myself. I found myself in a long distance telephone call to her.

"Honey, I don't know if anything happened to you like that. Maybe nothing did. I hope not. But I know things happened to me and I didn't even remember them, and yet now I know it was having a lot of impact on my life whether I knew it or not. And I just want you to know that if it happened, or if you ever remember anything like that, you can tell me. I don't care if it's twenty years from now, or if it was your father, grandfather, brother, aunt — whoever. It might hurt terribly to hear it, but I love you, and I want you to know you can always tell me."

I think about what I could allow myself to see and know when they were children, and I wonder. I haven't talked to Dave about this yet, but I'm going to.

One of the most powerful things Inie did for my kid was to say "It's O.K. You can talk about it here." Even though my own babies are grown adults now, I want no less for them if they need it.

If you love someone who's facing all this — be gentle. Be kind and patient, especially if you're in a sexual relationship. Try to understand. If you truly loved a recovering alcoholic, would you demand they accompany you to a bar to prove they love you? Well, that incest or sexual abuse victim you love may just have to reclaim new levels of control over his or her own body in order to become a survivor. Hang in and trust the process. Allow room for growth and healing. If you need help, get that, too.

Finally I'd like to offer some advice to anyone who's facing the issue of sexual abuse in their own life.

Above all, get every bit of good, competent support you need.

You did not ask for this item to be on your life's agenda, and it's not your fault you're stuck with it. You deserve help and the time it takes to work this out.

Look around for help. Check with the local women's center if you have one. Ask about who's good and experienced in this issue or have somebody do it for you.

Some of that help may need to be professional. As Sue said, this is pretty heavy stuff. But make sure your helper is one who will deal with this issue. One recent study showed that nearly half of American women were sexually abused in childhood, and the numbers are also high for men. While this means we are not alone in our struggle, it also says that surely this number includes a lot of therapists who are somehow affected, either as victims themselves, or with someone they love having been a victim. While some will have dealt with their own struggles, many will not have. We — the professional helping community — cannot help others with what we cannot face ourselves.

Some of the best help on this issue can come from non-professionals in such efforts as support groups. I did a study in graduate school of adult incest survivors, and the ones who were doing the best had made the most contact with other survivors — especially survivors who were facing their own pain. It was damned hard to go to the first incest support group meeting, but it was one of the best things I did for myself. It really helped me solidify my own recovery process.

All this takes time. I fought it all the way but it's critical to hang in and take the time to heal and learn. I truly see myself as a ''recovering person'' as much as if I were shaking off the effects of drugs or a severe disease. I'm allowing myself time to recover. I'd suggest it's a good rule of thumb to not make any huge life changes during early parts of recovery. Take time. Let yourself heal.

There is no magic/dramatic ending. New layers of this stuff still come to the surface for me and demand attention. And I know that's true for other survivors, too. But over time, the calm, productive spaces get longer, and the upheavals get shorter and are more quickly dealt with.

If this is something you need to deal with, I can only offer the following general formula.

Make the commitment to deal with it, completely, no matter what.

Get all the support and help you need.

Get a good hold on your nerve and stay with it. Take time. Easy does it.

Love yourself more than you ever have before. You need it.

Beyond that, life has it's ups and downs, and somehow it goes on. Don't kill yourself. You deserve more than that. There's no big ending as near as I can tell. You move into a better, more comfortable and happy phase, and it lightens up if you hang with it. Trust the process.

And that's it, I guess.

As I write this last paragraph, the sun is shining, I have people who love me and I love them. I work as best I know how, I care, and I deal with things as they come. I am alive. And I love me. That's pretty neat.

Take care.

FIVE YEARS LATER

I don't know if it is ever totally over
It's always there.
I can't trade my childhood in for another
And then go on like all this never happened.

It is more like a wound that has been cauterized
Or like a sore that has been lanced,
And drained,
And then carefully dressed with medications,
And treated with tender care
Until it healed.
Deeply.
From the inside out.
And now is the time when the air clears after a battle,
When the dust has settled,
And the smell of burned flesh and hair has drifted

And given way to fresher, cleaner air.
This is when as a weary battler, you can look about
And realize that even though this terrible event happened,
That this day, too will have a normal sunset.
Life goes on.

If at one time these memories, this pain, was repressed,
It is now re-repressed.
In a new and healthier way.
There is now more space in me to simply live my life,
From day to day.
Easy does it.
I can go for weeks without thinking of it.
And if I hurt now it is almost always
For the real events of my life today.
At times the old pain will ooze up in me
And if it does, it is apt to be some hidden, unexplored,
   unresolved, thought
Which, like a stone in my shoe,
Nags to be removed.
I am much better at that kind of maintenance now
Like a patient who has learned the warning signs of cancer,
I do not treat the old pain lightly
As if it were only a zit on my nose.

I am a recovering person/an emotional diabetic.
I live a managed life to some extent.
That means there are certain situations I do not allow
   myself to be in,
For my kid's sake,
And for mine.
And then, like a well cared for child,
It leaves the rest of my life for me to simply live and enjoy.

I have, with careful help,
Reclaimed my soul,
And my responsibility now
Is to go on with my life.
And our responsibility together, you and I,
Is to help save as many others as we can along the way.

THERAPIST'S AFTERWORD

"The basic strategy of the new experiential psychotherapy requires that, to achieve the best therapeutic result, both therapist and client suspend as much as possible their conceptual framework, anticipations and expectations during the experiential process. Both should be open and adventurous, ready to follow the flow of experience with a deep trust that the organism will find its own way to heal itself and evolve."

> Fritjof Capra
> The Turning Point
> 1982, p. 387

When Kathy and I met in the fall of 1981, we had both been deeply affected by the Civil Rights Movement as well as the Women's Movement. I felt a strong necessity to incorporate what I believed and had discovered into my work as a therapist. The personal, I knew, is also political. I had grown to feel that therapy is about setting free, not about leading along. It is about trusting one's self, and trusting one's client's self. It is about admitting that I know very little, and about creating a safe place for someone to feel and experience whatever emerges in the natural process of healing, no matter what form it takes, no matter how intense it becomes. It is about helping unlock aborted, boxed-in experiences, so they can move towards completion, their energy freed and turned constructive. It is about listening to the irrational and the symbolic, to dreams and messages from the place where we know more than we know that we know. It is about helping to overcome our fears and resistances that block our inner process, and life as it goes on. Therapy is about facing fear, my own and the client's, as also real, as part of living, as often justified. It is about learning what we are capable of, ranging from murder to creative ecstasy. Above all, it is about becoming a choice-maker and taking responsibility for one's life. All this I felt and feel strongly. I also thought I was pretty liberal. Kathy taught me a lot about being pale-faced and naive, about being middle class, and about raw emotions. I thank her for that; she has helped me grow.

My training has been eclectic. I am indebted to many people, so much so that it is hard to know anymore who to mention. If I mention one, it should be Carl Jung. He saw our organism as self-regulatory, self-healing, and self-transcending. He believed that the right way to wholeness is made up of fateful detours and wrong turnings. He saw our inner "demons" as highly charged complexes, wounds encapsulated for survival's sake, stopping the inner flow or "running us," all the while calling out to be freed through their very actions of disruption.

Jung, being a man of his time, was sometimes sexist. At the same time he wrote as early as 1927 "the modern woman stands before a great cultural task which means, perhaps, the beginning of a new era". Perhaps most important of all he taught me that the task of a therapist is to be a midwife helping her clients give birth to themselves. It gave me a basic orientation that feels like a fit.

During the nine months (!) I worked with Kathy I did not make any notes. I respected my client's apprehension of being in a file, available to "god knows who". Besides, Kathy made her own notes as she tried to reflect on what happened in our weekly sessions. It made my note taking less necessary. Though it did not always feel that way to her, the was in charge of the process, even in that respect.

Now three years later I wish I had written down something, not because it would have improved the process, because I don't think it needed that at the time, but because I would be able to recall in more detail what was happening on my side of this intense process as we went through it. Perhaps time has filtered out what was most important.

From the first session on I had a deep respect for this woman who had ''no choice but'' to put her head in my lap, whose kid came to me stuttering, needing to be heard in a desperate attempt to make a bridge; scared to death but determined to live, wanting to come out of the box, wanting to leave the ice floe on which she was slipping away again — old wounds ripped open. I had respect for her survival strength — the fact that she survived at all, and had become an active strong woman in the community, an excellent tennis player, a top student, a warm human being with a marvelous sense of humor. We had very few sessions that did not end in a releasing laugh. She had dignity, honesty, and unbelievable energy. She had no choice but to let her kid explore her raw feelings and her ''embarrassingly'' strong needs, but the adult never relinquished her independence.

In a way Kathy's journey reminds me of the journey of Ayla in Jean Auel's *The Clan of the Cave Bear* and *The Valley of Horses*. Ayla was a Neolithic orphan found by members of the Clan of the Cave Bear, part of a Cro-Magnon culture in prehistoric Europe. Ayla's appearance was different, to the clan she was ugly. Her capacity for communicating, her ability to think, her ability to cry was threatening and baffling to her adoptive family who devalued her and limited what she could do because she was a woman. She persisted against all odds, developing her skills (sometimes in secret) until she was declared ''dead'' by the Clan. Stricken with grief yet driven by her intelligence, her curiosity and her destiny, she left the community and explored where the Clan never dared to travel.

Like Ayla, Kathy often expressed that she did not understand where she came from; that she felt ugly, different, "the other" most of her life. In search of family she imagined Aunt Ruth, and fantasized belonging to distant relatives who had left generations ago for the West. Once she dreamed that her kid was contentedly asleep, sucking her thumb, in her grandfather's trunk. (Her grandfather died at the railroad station and the trunk never made it to the West where he was heading.) Kathy imagined folks who could understand her and guide her, teach her and love her. At a very young age she had "knowledge" of exciting possibilities in herself; yet all the while she felt alien and unwanted, not understood, often ostracized, ridiculed and abused. Like Ayla she was punished for her insight and the threat it imposed. Like Ayla she was driven to push on, strengthen herself, find her own way guided by a strong intellect, intuition, and survival instinct. Like Ayla she found sustenance in the beauty of nature so abundant in the rural area where she grew up. The earth as mother gave her a cradle that saved her life.

Indian tradition teaches about being part of the age old rhythms. She was drawn to the Indian in her and identified with the suffering of Native Americans. But even there she did not totally belong; too brown to be white, too white to be red. The final quest of Ayla, the mythic heroine, was to find others like herself. Like her contemporary counterparts in women's struggle today, Ayla had, time and again to decide what she had to do in the face of opposition and danger. She had to be strong but she yearned, against all odds, for love and the communal aspects of life. I see Kathy's struggle as a uniquely personal, painful version, a much larger one of which we all are a part. Perhaps it is in this search that we *are* all kin.

Kathy's book speaks for itself. It tells her story, her struggle with incest and physical abuse, and her courageous process to become whole, to heal. I had the privilege to be her midwife, although it did not always feel like a privilege. I, too, dreaded the sessions.

I never knew quite what would be next: her kid called the shots a lot of the time. Much of the therapy was intensive listening to the kid telling her story, reliving her pain.

Often I had to encourage her, letting her know that it was O.K. to break the conspiracy of silence. The taboo on telling was incredibly strong from the beginning. When you are little and threatened with a knife on your chest to make you be quiet, it is hard to break through that. The kid was distrustful, anxious, angry, terrified, and feisty at the same time. Invariably, in each session there would be a short struggle on Kathy's side to remain composed, to stay in her adult. Invariably that struggle was in vain. Some bodily tension would intensify: in her stomach, her chest her vaginal or rectal area, her thighs or her legs. I would encourage her to "let it happen" and she would surrender and plunge into what perhaps can best be described as a spontaneous trance state, a going into the level of consciousness where her kid-complex resides. She would become the kid in the middle of intense agony, banging her head in an attempt to silence the terror but inevitably going full fledged into a past experience. Often I had to protect her from hurting herself; I was not always successful. My room was quite small. She could hurt herself on the table or the bookcase or by banging on the floor. I felt lucky that I was quite strong and could match her muscle strength, because the kid lived in an unmistakably adult body.

The next problem was to try to figure out what was going on for the kid. Much of it was non-verbal and I had to be very keen on body language so I could tune in, respond, challenge, and, most of all, comfort her as she was reliving her ordeals and the emotions that came with it. I had to assure her that it was not her fault, that she was indeed lovable. (Something I strongly felt.) I had to let her know that I knew it hurt, that she had a right to be angry, to cry and to be scared. More than anything else I had to validate her experience, so she did not have to go back in the box where she had been locked up for so long.

Those moments were very intense: I was not always sure where my responses came from. I learned to trust my "bones" because there was not much else I could rely on. Sometimes I knew exactly what was happening for her, sometimes I could only guess.

After a while she would be obviously spent, but still in a trance state. I would talk to her in that state, stressing that she would remember everything when she woke up so we could talk about it, or so she could process it in her own way, write about it, take it further. (The first two times I did not stress the remembering, but I quickly learned how important that was.) Then I suggested to her to hold the kid so she could calm down, feel warm and safe and cared for. The caring felt crucial for two reasons. First, because the kid needed that and had never experienced it before. Secondly, Kathy needed to learn to "become her own mother", to accept and love the battered part of herself so it could grow and become a productive integrated part, of her.

It also felt important to minimize her dependency on me. Obviously we were in a reparenting process. It felt important that the adult in her had an active role in that process from the beginning.

Again I would stress that she would remember, not only everything that had happened while in a trance, but also everything I had said. I wanted to make sure that she had all the information. She had a right to know. After it seemed certain that the kid was comforted I would slowly take her out of the trance state the way one takes people out of a hypnotic state. I would emphasize that she would feel relaxed and energized in an attempt to minimize the effects of the emotional turmoil and the thrashing around. I would usually bring her closer and closer to coming back and suggest that she would wake up when I would hold her hand. At one time I decided to try to let her come out of the trance at her own pace. Usually time, if not anything else, pressed me to actively bring her out myself.

After a while I wondered whether perhaps this way I was creating dependence that neither Kathy nor I wanted. So I suggested that she come out on her own account when she was ready. The result was that she became very panicky. The kid was afraid to be left in that place alone, as had happened when she was a child. I ended up reassuring her and bringing her back myself. It showed me that I could push too hard, that she still needed the assurance that the trip down-in was safe. I had to follow the process. Besides, I soon learned that Kathy would fight if I became too directive. She describes in her book how she once fought my trying to set the agenda, even though it was based on written stuff she had left with me the last time around.

In the beginning Kathy's writing was the thread that connected our sessions. We had very little time to talk as adult to adult on the conscious level. Her writing was intense and hard work, and a crucial part of the therapy. It also kept me informed as to what was going on for her, what she remembered, what she was digesting, and what she was struggling with.

The process went with spurts and relapses, but the kid grew younger and younger until she almost seemed a baby (judging by her perceptions of the size of the crib she was in or the size of a hand touching her). She went all the way back to her first terrifyingly ambivalent experiences when she naturally called out for the comfort of a mother, who at the same time incomprehensibly posed the gravest threat to her well being.

Gradually the calm between periods of tension and turmoil grew larger and larger. The kid in Kathy began to grow again and to explore. Her life was opening up, and the kid now posed different problems: what do you do with a kid who does not want to stay at work, who wants to suck her thumb, who just wants to ride in the car and look around, who is approaching adolescence and growing sexually?

All through the process Kathy was mothering her kid, or it is perhaps more correct to say that we together were reparenting her kid. One thing that she desperately needed to experience was that it was possible to be held, to be loved, without sexual exploitation. Time and again she would ask me, ''please don't touch me the way my mother did.'' The adult was embarrassed by the distrust of the kid, the kid simply had to make sure and test me again and again. When the tension in her body would mount, previous to going into the level where the kid was, I had to be very careful not to touch her. I had to stay close to her so I could protect her physically when needed, but if I accidentally touched her she would jump in terror. Afterwards, when spent, I would touch her freely like one does a child and/or an adult friend. That, too, was an important and natural part of the process.

One of the most critical times came when Kathy was working through a period when her kid (child) was suicidal. She dreamed about her little girl floating face down in the creek running though her parents' land; the water red with blood, her arms cut off. It shook her to the core. The despair of the kid was unbearable, and the adult was terrified that she would take her own life. The Talwin lured her, but aggravated the terror. In despair she brought the Talwin to me. I took it because she wanted that safeguard, but I let her know that it was there for the asking. I knew full well that if she wanted to kill herself there were many other ways to do it.

I had a deep trust that she would not choose that road. The whole process seemed a contraindication to that, but I could not be totally sure and Kathy was afraid of her kid. I could have advised her to commit herself, but I felt then and now that commitment would have been a crucial mistake, a vote of no confidence, the last thing the kid needed. It did seem important that the adult and the kid knew I was there, accessible by phone, and that I trusted and respected the process, and most of all that I cared.

Perhaps tranquilizers or an antidepressant could have given some relief. I have no authority to prescribe those but somebody else could have. It would have taken the edge off for sure, but taking the edge off her intense feeling very likely would dull her to the natural healing process that was taking place. I did not want to risk that, and Kathy did not ask for it. It was after that very session in which Kathy brought me the Talwin that she wrote: "Today with Inie, I felt I really held my kid. For the first time she leaned on me a little more as if she trusted me. And I liked it." It was, for me, confirmation that we were on the right track.

All through the process Kathy struggled with what she perceived as the inequality of the situation. She was aware that the adult her and the adult me were equal, and it was embarrassing to her that this kid took over and spoiled the potential of a friendship. How could I respect her? Besides, what did she really know about me? All this was complicated by our cultural differences: I, white middle class with a Dutch Calvinist background; and she, part Indian with strong gut level working class emotions, and a justified distrust of where I was coming from. The truth is that not only did I respect her, she sometimes intimidated me with her enormous energy and quick wit and her ability as a writer. At the same time, some form of inequality was inherent in our process for a while. At first the relationship was mostly between the adult me and her shaky, frenzied kid, and only slowly was there more space for us adult women to get to know each other.

Looking back, our connection was truly multi-leveled. Jung stated that in real therapy neither the client nor the therapist stays the same. I have found this to be very true. It was not only her kid who grew, mine grew too, and became more alive and open and real. I grew professionally, but also as a person. In a way I simply had to rise to the occasion. Often I came out of our sessions exhausted, feeling stripped to the bone sometimes, but centered and very human.

What has all this to do with other incest survivors? I feel it is of utmost importance that one who has been there, who also happens to be a good writer, tells her story. The client's story is more important than the story of the therapist; too often that focus is turned around.

Carl Rogers made the observation, in *On Becoming A Person* that "what is most personal is most general". When one expresses oneself in ways that are so uniquely personal that one feels that probably no one else will understand, that is exactly when one speaks most deeply to others. It is important to add here the truth that emerged from women's consciousness raising groups: "the personal is the political." The taboo has been broken. Finally something is being done, it is not yet nearly enough.

At the same time, circumstances are not the only determinants that shape us. What we do with these circumstances is crucial to the outcome. Why some people survive the unthinkable while others collapse for close to no reason at all has puzzled many. Victor Frankl describes, in his book *Man's Search for Meaning*, his experiences as a Jew in a Nazi concentration camp. He observed that some people submitted and succumbed quickly, while others used their imagination and stretched their endurance to the limit. Focusing on some mission, some purpose for which they felt they were intended to live, a proportionately large number managed to survive.

Jean Bolen in her book *Goddesses in Everywoman* notes how she met people in her practice with childhoods full of deprivation, cruelty, beatings, and sexual abuse, who, despite it all did not become abusers (as would be expected), but instead were people who felt compassion for others. In both the child and the later adult, an essence of trust, a sense of self, and a capacity for love and hope survived. They were wounded, small and powerless, but from an early age they refused to be victims. Each had an inner myth, a fantasy life or imaginary companions to sustain them.

Kathy clearly belongs to the survivors. Her kid was deeply wounded but she also had the makings of a heroine (like Ayla). She imagined her "Aunt Ruth" who would not allow her to hate

186

her mother; who taught her a sense of humor and the wonders of art and literature, who encouraged her to go to college, and who believed she could be a writer someday.

The fact that Kathy is a survivor does not mean that her pain was less, or that she was less in need of healing. It did mean that she was willing to endure the hardship of therapy and not give up.

Finally I would like to share some things that have struck me as important during the process with Kathy (and other incest survivors as well), that can perhaps be of help to other therapists.

(1) All incest survivors I have worked with are struggling with the "wounded child" in themselves. Jung encourages us to personalize and perhaps name the different forces in ourselves, the different parts of ourselves, as we naturally do in dreams. This personalization gives us a tool to become more aware, to listen, to dialogue, to affirm, to nurture, and to be challenged by those forces that either were left behind and boxed in of necessity a long time ago, or that only now become ready to be actualized in our process of individuation. Kathy, as is the case with many clients, knew this instinctively. She had already written about the little person housed in her chest before she knew me. We "know" what is the best method for our healing process. Kathy's example proves that.

The tool of personalization gives us an active role in our process, and helps us step by step to transform ourselves from victims into survivors and choicemakers. In Kathy's case the kid was a very vivid personalization who was there right from the start as a little person needing to be reckoned with. I actively encouraged that. The kid is not always so obviously there from the beginning. It is often embarrassing to clients to admit such an unstable presence. The kid is often condemned. The client needs permission to feel free to express the kid, to break the taboo of silence imposed a long time ago.

(2) The first session is often crucial. In Kathy's case, something happened between her kid and me that was far more important than a lengthy intake interview to gather information or an attempt at diagnosis could have been. The latter probably would have scared her away. I was drawn to intensely listen to, and reassure the wounded child, and she felt heard and safe. It is important that the therapist is willing to encourage and support a healing journey without fully understanding it. When the client chooses to be in our office, there is already a process underway that we need to trust and facilitate.

(3) To the client, especially when she starts remembering what happened to her as a child, this process often feels like going crazy. Generally incest survivors who come to us are not going crazy, but they need reassurance that they are not. They need to know they are on a healing trip instead, and that we trust that trip. If we do not trust it, we must not fake it as a therapeutic technique. Any feelings that do not come from our own core are unreal and untherapeutic. They become easily manipulative and betray the client, often with disastrous result.

To trust the process does not mean that we should trust it blindly. The therapist needs to stay alert, like a midwife, to possible complications, while all the while remaining aware that the organism basically knows how to give birth, how to heal. To respect this ''inner wisdom'' of the client also means that there are times when resistance needs to be taken seriously. To bring on labor artificially, to push (instead of facilitating) can be violating. Some may never be ready to face ''all.'' Who are we to decide that they should?

Sometimes the messages are confusing and contradictory. Kathy's ''adult'' told me at one time ''get tough with me, please, let's do it and be done''. During the same time the messages from her kid ranged all the way from ''I don't need you, I don't need anybody—don't touch me, I will hit you, I will. You will be sorry'' to ''please, be careful with me.'' The latter felt like a true communication.

(4) During the time that memories come back, it is helpful if work stress can be minimized somewhat. This is not always possible and it was not possible in Kathy's case; it is one of the things that made her process extremely demanding. At the same time it is important to realize that work and/or a daily routine to focus on is crucially important. It provides time out, and helps to keep the head above water, preventing the ego from being overwhelmed. The reality of a daily routine and/or work requires a balancing act that is helpful.

(5) From the first day on, Kathy fell spontaneously into a trance-

like state in which she relived her childhood experiences. She chose, or to stay truer to what she felt, "something in her" chose this route. She used the same spontaneous method Anna 0. had used when working with Breuer at the end of the 19th century. It was this experience that led Freud to the discovery of the unconscious and the development of psychoanalysis.

Anna 0. (her real name was Bertha Pappenheim) was virtually abandoned by Breuer, who could not handle, and at the time did not understand, the transference situation. Anna, after an initial worsening of her condition following the break with Breuer, recouped and later in life became an active social worker and feminist in Germany. Her healing process was perhaps damaged for a while by the traumatic interruption, but it was not permanently thwarted. She "knew" what she needed in order to heal, but she needed someone who would not "freak out" and who could handle the transference situation to do it. Knowing about this helped me trust what was happening with Kathy.

(6) A whole array of transference feelings (love, fear, anger, guilt, distrust, shame, sex, and so on) was played out between Kathy and me. We were both strongly concerned about keeping the feelings between the kid and her "mother-figure" and the two adults separate. It is crucial for the therapist to be trustworthy this way. It is tempting to feel like the "great therapist", or to take negative feelings personally, or to use one's power the wrong way. Transference feelings are often intensified when trance states are involved. Kathy's sense of humor and her feisty kid also helped me to keep seeing things clearly.

(7) Not everybody chooses spontaneous trance. For Kathy it was the main channel through which she accomplished her goal. Others may have a strong resistance to "letting it happen" that way, or different channels may be preferred naturally. Dreams played a role in Kathy's process, but have played a much larger role in work with others. Because the experiences happened during childhood (sometimes during a preverbal period), it is important to focus on feelings and tensions in the different parts of the

body where experiences are stored. Eugene Gendlin's process of "focusing" has been helpful at times, so have visualization, spontaneous writing, and drawing. Personally, I have not tried active hypnosis. I have been (perhaps too much so) afraid to disturb the spontaneous process. In general, I would encourage everyone to listen to the client, and perhaps try what they do best.

(8) The issues around sexuality are particularly sensitive for the incest survivor. The adult should never be pushed farther than what the kid is able to handle. The spontaneous development of her sexuality and her own pace of discovery have been violated in the past. Sex is often associated with confusion and abuse. The kid was often overstimulated. Some of the ways she experienced her sexuality may have become loaded with feelings of terror. In many cases there is a split between the experience of love and sex that makes it hard to be sexual with those the incest survivor loves most.

To be sexually vulnerable, or even to experience the genital area exposed, as during a gynecological examination, can be extremely frightening. Therapist and client need to allow the kid to express those feelings no matter what they are.

A sexual partner who is willing to listen and not push can be extremely helpful in the healing process.

(9) The format that evolved naturally for Kathy and me was to work in weekly three hour mini-marathon sessions. I am not sure it could have been done in any other way by Kathy or by myself. It definitely enhanced the intensity and speed of the process as a whole. The fifty minute therapy hour is sometimes a needed structure, sometimes an obstacle. If at all possible, I recommend flexibility in this respect.

I would like to give the practical warning that it is important to safeguard the client against hurting herself during the process of recalling and reliving. Fortunately I could match Kathy's strength. If you cannot do that, it becomes doubly important to have space and lots of pillows available.

(10) If I had to single out one thing that is of the utmost importance to the incest survivor, I would emphasize the importance of the validation of her experience. When she works through her confusion, isolation, and disturbed perception of reality, the one thing she needs to hear time and again is that it was not her fault, that she did not make it happen, that she did not deserve it, and that there was nothing wrong with her. Disturbingly common messages from adults to abused children have been "you must be imagining it" or "you must be asking for it." The latter is a ludicrous statement considering the power of a little child. The first statement has been unfortunately reinforced by Freud's psychoanalytic theory of the Oedipus complex and its emphasis on childhood sexual fantasy.

After at first discovering many instances of incestuous abuse among his patients, and believing these to be the major cause of their problems, Freud changed his mind. In *"An Autobiographical Study"* he writes ". . . . I was at last obliged to recognize that these scenes of seduction had never taken place, and that they were only fantasies which my patients had made up. . . When I had pulled myself together, I was able to draw the right conclusion from my discovery: namely that the neurotic symptoms were not related directly to actual events but to wishful fantasies. . . ." For a long time this change of mind in Freud has conditioned the professional to doubt rather than validate the client's experience, and the odds have been stacked against the kid's perceptions by layman and professional alike. We have to face the uncomfortable truth that Freud's early discoveries were closer to the reality than his later conclusions. "Wishful fantasies" does not fit as a description of the relived horror and confusion recalled with so much dread.

(11) In conjunction with (or as a follow up or alternative to) individual therapy, working in a group can be extremely helpful to the incest survivor. It was to Kathy. The sharing of similar issues, experiences, and anxieties breaks the sense of isolation in a way that individual therapy cannot. The alternating roles of helper and helpee prevent the sense of humiliation that might evolve from being the helpee only. For many people, however, individual work

remains important. Therapist and client need to find the right balance in this respect.

(12) If it happens that you are a therapist and an incest survivor yourself, the pain of going through a process like this with somebody else can be enormous. On one hand, the fact that you have been there helps. On the other hand, certain parts of the process may hit way too close for comfort. Your own kid may get very upset, additional memories may come up for you, or you may get caught in anger. If this is the case, a back-up therapist (or trusted person to talk to) and honesty, is crucial for you as well as your client.

Helen Epstein, in *Children of the Holocaust*, describes how the children of survivors are deeply affected by the harsh fate their parents had undergone in the past. Even if those parents are strong, have created the best circumstances for their offspring and tried to "live on", these children are still controlled by the facts and feelings that have been carefully locked away. It is important for the sake of the wounded and for the sake of their children as well, to expose the wound, to experience and to articulate, so that healing can take place.

We touch each other on conscious as well as unconscious levels. Helen Epstein writes about parents and children, but to a greater or lesser extent the same is true for any intense relationship. The relationship between therapist and client is no exception.

I am fortunate that I was not physically or sexually abused as a child. In working with clients those "buttons" are not pushed for me (although other "buttons" are). However, working with survivors who are also therapists has taught me that the issues of transference and counter transference as described above, can become acutely intense in such a situation. We have the responsibility to work through these issues. As therapists, we are inclined to demand a total effort from our clients. This demand only works if we are aware that it also applies to ourselves.

All through the process Kathy hated the therapy. She wanted it to be "over with" NOW, but time and again her inner process relentlessly pushed her on. She was not alone in her ambivalent feelings. I too wanted it to be over with, for her sake and for my sake.

Through reading her book I realize that a few times wishful thinking made me say something that perhaps prematurely conveyed a sense of "we have arrived." One day Kathy asked me to physically hold the sweater/kid. She wanted someone else to lovingly hold the kid before she would no longer be there as a separate little human being inside. She needed to establish that memory because she felt the kid slowly changing and growing and becoming a more organic part of herself. When I did as she asked we were both deeply moved, and I said "I think you have made it—the kid's made it; I think you and the kid are one person now." I wanted so much to believe that, and I wanted her to believe that. However, it would have been more accurate, and perhaps more helpful, if I had said "I think you are making it—the kid is making it, I think you and the kid are becoming more one person now". I don't think Kathy took my statement as the gospel truth (she never did anyway), but through working with her it came home to me even more strongly that healing is an ongoing process.

It is probably not possible to ever totally erase the past. Healing means that the past does not "run" us anymore like it used to. Becoming "whole" means we are less and less split inside so we can more and more put our energy into living fully. But the old pain can still be triggered occasionally, often by events we have no control over. If this happens at a time that the client has the impression that she is totally "cured", she is in for a tremendous downer and panic will strike. She needs to be forewarned that those old "nerve connections" are still there and can be activated at times (that the kid can still easily get upset). But she also needs to know that now she has the tools to take care of herself, to figure out what called forth her reaction and then to manage the situation without feeling defeated. In some cases it is helpful to go back to the therapist. Kathy has done that sporadically. Often one session proved enough, and those sessions have become fewer and farther between.

Perhaps healing at its very core comes down to respecting the truth as it emerges for both client and therapist. Kathy certainly did not go for less. I thank her for trusting me.

Inie Bijkerk